BREAKTHROUGH

120 UNCOMMON PRAYERS FOR BUSINESS EXECUTIVES

GREAT EZENWOKS

Copyright © 2024 by Great Ezenwoks
All rights reserved. No part of this publication may be Reproduced, stored or transmitted in any form or by any Means, electronic, mechanical, photocopying, recording, Scanning, or otherwise without written permission from the Publisher.
It is illegal to copy this book, post it to a website, or distribute it by any other means without permission.

Table of Contents

Introduction _____ 6
1. The Entrepreneurial Spirit: Prayers for Vision and Boldness _____ 10
2. Miracle-Working Prayers for Business Growth _____ 19
3. Commanding Favor and Increase in the Marketplace _____ 27
4. Overcoming Obstacles and Breaking Through Barriers _____ 36
5. Prophetic Prayers to Seize New Opportunities _____ 44
6. Birthing New Ideas and Innovations _____ 57
7. Speaking Prosperity and Abundance into Existence _____ 59
8. Attracting an Overflow of Clients and Customers _____ 67
9. Supernatural Wisdom for Strategic Decision-Making _____ 75

10. Building a Kingdom-Minded Company Culture___83
11. Praying for Excellence and Peak Performance___91
12. Defeating the Spirit of Lack and Limitation___107
13. Prayers for Harmonious Partnerships and Teamwork___107
14. Breaking Generational Curses of Failure___115
15. Commanding Doors to Open Internationally___122
16. Unstoppable Prayers for Influence and Impact___130
17. Pleading the Blood for Protection and Security___138
18. Commanding Angels to Assist in Business Affairs___147
19. Rebuking Satanic Harassment in the Workplace___155
20. Praying for Explosive Sales and Profitability___165

21. Birthing New Streams of Income and Wealth___170
22. Releasing Blessings on Employees and Leaders___177
23. Prayers for Work-Life Balance and Priorities___191
24. Overcoming Anxiety, Stress and Burnout___197
25. Consecrating Business for Kingdom Purposes___203
Conclusion: From Prayers to Powerhouse Performance___210

INTRODUCTION

In a fiercely competitive global marketplace, the difference between success and failure can hinge on the prayers of men and women with an insatiable hunger to see God's supernatural power manifested in their businesses and careers. Breakthrough isn't just the title of this book - it's the rallying cry for a generation of entrepreneurs and leaders who refuse to accept mediocrity or settle for average results.

As a business executive, your daily routine is likely filled with high-stakes decisions, relentless deadlines, and intense pressure to meet targets and produce outstanding financial performance. In such a demanding environment, it's easy to feel overwhelmed, make fear-based choices, or succumb to stress and burnout. But you were created for more than mere survival - you were fashioned for dominion!

This book **120 Uncommon Prayers for Business Executives** provides you with a powerful spiritual weapon to break out of constricting patterns and propel your business into new dimensions of success, abundance, and influence. Crafted from Scriptural principles, these prayers will help you:

- **Boldly birth creative ideas and innovations**
- **Attract more customers/clients than you can handle**
- **Experience a resurrection of dead opportunities**

- Unlock the flow of wisdom for critical decisions
- Break through ceilings and obstacles once and for all
- Unleash angelic forces to assist in the marketplace
- And much more!

Whether you pray through this book systematically or grab it as a reference manual when facing specific business issues, you will find yourself armed with focused, authoritative declarations that release Heaven's resources into your career and open new realms of Kingdom impact.

The prayers in this book aren't formulaic or dry - they are passionate pleas infused with prophetic power to demolish limiting thought patterns and reset the spiritual atmosphere over your work environment. They are uttered with a violence that smashes satanic opposition and clears away obstacles. With every syllable, you are mounting an offensive assault against the status quo!

Business executives around the world are experiencing breakthroughs, accelerating past their competition, and leaving average performers in the dust. They are unstoppable because they have tapped into a superior Source of wisdom, favor, and supply.

Reader, the same is available to you! Buckle your seatbelt and get ready, because the breakthrough you've been awaiting is contained in these explosive prayers. Prepare for the miraculous as you pray in faith - nothing will be impossible for you!

CHAPTER 1
THE ENTREPRENEURIAL SPIRIT: PRAYERS FOR VISION AND BOLDNESS

From the opening chapters of Genesis, Scripture reveals that God designed humanity to cultivate creation through entrepreneurial endeavors marked by vision, courage, and relentless innovation. God's first recorded directive to Adam was to "be fruitful and multiply; fill the earth and subdue it" (Genesis 1:28). This clarion call launched humanity's sacred responsibility as vice-regents to steward the earth's vast potential through pioneering enterprises that would solve problems, meet needs, and expand God's Kingdom footprint across the globe.

The entrepreneurial spirit is the very essence of this bold, adventurous assignment. It's the intrepid force that drove Noah to construct history's first shipbuilding company, equipping him to navigate uncharted waters during the Flood. It's the fuel that empowered Abraham to become a wealthy wandering entrepreneur who amassed great possessions through livestock, business dealings, and strategic property acquisitions in new lands. Jacob continued this trailblazing spirit by birthing new trade routes and agricultural techniques that established generational wealth and economic autonomy.

In modern times, the entrepreneurial spirit burns just as brilliantly in visionary leaders who have disrupted industries and reimagined entire markets. From the light bulb to the iPhone, advances that have transformed civilization often emerged from

the prayer-drenched dreams of entrepreneurs who dared to build what others dismissed as impossible fantasies.

In this chapter, we will travail through prophetic prayers that ignite fresh spiritual fire to your God-inspired visions and entrepreneurial ideas. Through these passionate petitions, you will break out of limiting mindsets and constricting boundaries that have kept your dreams in captivity. You will experience a rejuvenation of holy perseverance and unstoppable tenacity to press through obstacles and push into new territory, no matter the cost. These prayers will increase your capacity to risk everything in radical obedience to the Spirit's still, small voice beckoning you into breakthrough territory.

Key Lessons:
1. God Designed You for Entrepreneurial Dominion - You were fashioned in the very nature and image of the ultimate Entrepreneur - the Creator Himself. Refuse to settle for confinement or merely maintaining the status quo.

2. Prophetic Prayers Birth Visions and Kingdom Ideas - The most formidable weapon for unleashing a torrent of creative ideas and birthing visions is prophetic, Spirit-inspired prayers that demolish limiting mindsets.

3. Dream God-Sized Dreams That Demand Supernatural Help - Don't insult God with visions so small that you can accomplish them through human effort alone. Think exponentially bigger to necessitate divine intervention!

4. Feed Your Entrepreneurial Spirit Through Faith-Stretching Risks - Refuse to become complacent or comfortably domesticated. The entrepreneurial spirit thrives on calculated, Spirit-led risks that defy odds and probabilities.

5. Solve Problems That Expand God's Kingdom - At its core, your entrepreneurial vision should provide innovative solutions that make a transformational impact and advance God's sovereign agenda on the earth.

UNCOMMON PRAYERS
Prayer 1-10

1. I renounce the deadly sins of passivity, complacency, and small thinking that have kept my holy entrepreneurial dreams and Kingdom visions incarcerated. I break their power over my mind and declare freedom to dream big, God-inspired visions.

2. I command a revival of the ruthless, entrepreneurial spirit to burn within me with a holy desperation to establish God's dominion on earth through courageous endeavors that impact lives for eternity.

3. I demolish every self-imposed prison, confining box, and restrictive mindset that

has limited my capacity to conceive and give birth to innovative, God-inspired business ideas and Kingdom enterprises. I declare my mind is being renewed and expanded.

4. I lose a fresh anointing to operate in the realm of the Prophetic Seer. I decree the ability to have visions of future realities and dream God-sized dreams that demand supernatural intervention and stretch me far beyond my natural abilities.

5. I bind the spirit of fear, unbelief, and double-mindedness that has instilled hesitation, paralysis and inaction concerning launching new creative initiatives with powerful Kingdom impact. I reject inconsistency and wholeheartedly pursue God's purposes.

6. I decree a sovereign anointing of the entrepreneurial spirit to burn within me with the tenacious perseverance of the patriarchs Abraham, Isaac and Jacob - unwilling to quit until promises are completed, no matter how long it takes or how hot the furnace of testing.

7. I command a fresh impartation of the bold, courageous faith that marked the father of entrepreneurship - Abraham - who obeyed God without knowing where he was going. I will abandon all reliance on human wisdom and natural circumstances.

8. I lose the spirits of wisdom, innovation, creativity and divine ingenuity to impart God's insights and solutions for pioneering new initiatives that will strategically solve

complex challenges and transform societies worldwide.

9. I activate the spirit of influence like Joseph to gain sovereign favor, even in environments hostile to Kingdom advancement, so that I can have an unshakable, transcendent impact as a world-shaper for God's purposes.

10. I break generational curses of spiritual apathy, poverty mindsets, and failure to leave an entrepreneurial inheritance that impacts generations to come. I decree an impartation of an entrepreneurial legacy of visionary thinking that blesses my children and their children.

CHAPTER 2
MIRACLE-WORKING PRAYERS
FOR BUSINESS GROWTH

From cover to cover, the Scriptures reveal a God who delights in accelerating growth and miraculously multiplying ventures and resources far beyond natural constraints. When Jesus was confronted with limited provisions to feed a vast multitude, He didn't agonize or scale back - He expected the impossible! With just five loaves and two fish, His audacious prayers released multiplication that left 12 baskets full of leftovers after feeding over 5,000 people (Matthew 14).

God's capacity to supernaturally propel growth didn't stop with the Bible's completion. Throughout modern history, He has demonstrated the same penchant for miraculous increase and market dominance through Spirit-led entrepreneurs and leaders. From best-selling books that skyrocketed to the top of the charts through a divine marketing campaign, to fledgling companies that mushroomed into global titans within a decade, the annals of business are replete with testimonies that defy odds and possible explanations.

In this chapter, you'll wage spiritual warfare through prayers that activate miracle-working physics and set unrestrained growth into motion. No longer will you suffer under limiting patterns of incremental progress and slow-drip expansion. Instead, you'll unleash the same explosive growth trajectories witnessed throughout the Bible and history's most successful companies.

As you pray in faith, expect growth curves that demonstrate logarithmic upswings and vertical acceleration. Once stagnant or sluggish initiatives will suddenly burst with resurrection life as laws of rapid multiplication overtake former inertia. Closed doors will creak open, impossibly expanding your territory into new markets. Angelic hosts of economic acceleration and increase will be dispatched to undergird your breakthrough into increase and abundance.

The miracle-working prayers in this chapter storm the gateways of increase with the same raw faith and tenacity Abraham exhibited when hoping against hope for his barren wife to finally conceive (Romans 4:18). Each bold declaration prophetically declares what the spiritual realm will shortly birth into the natural realm concerning your finances, sales, resources, and overall expansion as an organization. Get ready - it's about to grow!

Key Lessons:
1. Expect Exponential, Not Incremental, Growth - Too often we shrink God down to manageable expectations of linear increase. Allow these prayers to recalibrate your capacity for explosive multiplication.

2. Nothing Is Too Difficult for God - Stop questioning how or if something can

happen. Meditate instead on how BIG it will be when your breakthrough manifests! There are no limits with our supernatural God.

3. Partner Your Faith with Prophetic Decrees - For miracles to manifest, you must boldly agree with the spiritual reality that already exists in Heaven and speak it forth with authority into the natural realm.

4. Engage the Support of Angels for Growth Angels are Spirit beings who await our prayers to assist with growing companies, expanding reach, accelerating favor, and guarding resources.

5. Approach Business with Holy Audacity - Like the boy who offered his paltry lunch to Jesus, offer what you have courageously to God, knowing He will multiply it exponentially beyond imagination!

UNCOMMON PRAYERS
Prayer. 11-20

11. I command the spiritual atmosphere over my business to be saturated with the anointing of increase and supernatural acceleration that transcends laws of incremental growth.

12. I lose a supernatural birthing and multiplication of sales at levels my company has never experienced before - overflowing, exponential, rapid expansion beyond my wildest projections.

13. I prophetically call forth resurrection power to quicken growth and breathe life into business areas that have remained stagnant, dormant or in decline. I decree explosive enlargement!

14. By faith, I decree open doors and Spirit-led connections that grant me access to new international markets and regions for unprecedented proliferation of my business.

15. I release angelic reinforcements of acceleration, favor, and increase to precede me and supernaturally position resources,

relationships, and opportunities essential for growth.

16. I cancel premature life-spans, forecasts of slow progress, and histories of momentum-killing delays that have prevented rapid advancement. I prophesy accelerated speed!

17. I command a baptism of bold, miracle-working faith like the Canaanite woman who persisted until her daughter was delivered and multiplied resources manifested (Matthew 15).

18. I bind the spirit of small-thinking, poverty mindsets, fear, unbelief and human skepticism from dictating limits to God's capacity to multiply streams of provision for growth.

19. I speak forth the favor and anointing for explosive business growth seen in the lives of biblical entrepreneurs like Abraham, Isaac, Jacob and Joseph. I receive their mantle!

20. I prophesy a violent overthrow of opposition voices that mock vision for growth, declaring, "Thus far you may come, but no farther! Here I take my stand!" (Job 38:11)

CHAPTER 3
COMMANDING FAVOR AND INCREASE IN THE MARKETPLACE

From the very inception of humanity's story, God designed His people to experience His superabundant favor resulting in exponential increase within the marketplace. When creating the first entrepreneurs - Adam and Eve - God blessed them with fruitfulness, multiplication, and dominion over the earth (Genesis 1:28). This foundational blessing established both the precedent and promise of supernatural favor propelling increase in whatever realm of industry and commerce His sons and daughters would operate.

As we study the lives of patriarchs like Abraham, Isaac, Jacob and Joseph, we witness God's covenant favor manifest through remarkable stories of explosive growth, prolific productivity, overflow and accumulation of vast wealth and resources. Despite personal flaws and failures, their bold faith and obedience activated a divine favor dynamic that caused increase to supernaturally chase and overtake them in business affairs, from flocks and herds to agricultural harvests and strategic property acquisitions.

But God's heart to release favor and increase did not stop with the Old Testament. The New Testament book of Acts opens with exponential increase as 3,000 souls are instantly added to the fledgling church through a supernatural outpouring of signs, wonders and miracles. Later, we see

supernatural favor allow the first believers to sell property and experience such substantial
overflow that there was no lack among them (Acts 4:33-34).

Across the centuries, this favor for wealth creation continued manifesting through

Christ-followers, from the Moravian missionaries who funded the Great Awakening through entrepreneurial business exploits, to giants of industry like John D. Rockefeller whose devoted giving helped fuel modern missions.

This powerful chapter will equip you to wage spiritual warfare to activate guaranteed favor and enabling for supernatural increase in the contemporary marketplace. The petitions will help you demolish obstacles, hindrances, and limiting mindsets that have kept you bound and struggling in cycles of lack. Instead, you'll unleash the faith to expect and command extravagant favor that causes you to be plowed over by torrents of overflow, abundance and blessing from the hand of the Lord!

Key Lessons

1. Supernatural Favor Produces Exponential Increase - From Genesis to today, God's plan is for His sons and daughters to walk in an extravagant anointing of favor that supernaturally multiplies every seed sown.

2. Favor Is a Covenantal Reality - Far from wishful thinking, walking in outrageous favor is your blood-bought covenant privilege through Christ's finished work on the cross.

3. God Uses Wealth for Kingdom Impact - Financial increase was never intended solely for personal accumulation but for funding Kingdom impact and advancing God's purposes globally.

4. Release Favor Through Authoritative Declarations - Like the centurion who released his faith through commanding

words, favor is activated and manifested through bold, prophetic decrees agreeing with Heaven.

5. Increase Often Comes Through Supernatural Means - Don't limit how God may release overflow into your life and business. Stay positioned for increase through miracles, angelic assistance or unexplainable happenings.

UNCOMMON PRAYERS
Prayers.21-30

21. Establishing a court case in Heaven's tribunals, I present the Blood of the

Everlasting Covenant that guarantees God's supernatural favor for exponential increase in the marketplace.

22. I declare powerful decrees demolishing every demonic assignment and generational curse attempting to obstruct, hinder, or erect obstacles to the manifestation of God's promised favor and overflow in my life and business endeavors.

23. Establishing the spiritual legal precedent of Abraham, Isaac, Jacob and Joseph as righteous heirs who operated in God's extravagant favor, I secure my inheritance

rights for the same blessing of multiplication and increase upon my seed and business affairs.

24. I bind the spirits of lack, poverty, struggle, insufficiency and finite mindsets that have limited my capacity to conceive and call forth the fullness of overflow and abundance that is mine by Covenant promise.

25. By faith, I loose and command the angelic hosts assigned to the storehouses of heaven's abundance to mobilize and come assist in accelerating financial increase, strategic relationships, resources, opportunities and market favor on my behalf.

26. Establishing the court case of definitive acceleration in Jesus' ministry on earth, His business was flooded with supernatural increase through miracles of multiplying limited resources into overabundance. I decree the same spiritual technology activating over my sphere.

27. Realizing the espoused Bride has been given access to the King's limitless riches through Union with Christ, I call forth the espousal blessings of the bride including multiplied influence, affluence, and the wealth of nations flooding into the family business.

28. As an Heir with Christ, I call the wealth from nations that have been heaping up for the righteous into my possession and available for Kingdom advancement and impact.

29. Through authoritative decrees, I prophetically create an atmosphere that supernaturally attracts and magnetizes favor for promotion, opportunity, contracts, clientele, and markets to be drawn to me and our organization.

30. I establish myself as a wise master builder, working Wisdom through my enterprises that produces wealth and positions me for the Proverbs 8 overflow where no good thing will be withheld from me.

CHAPTER 4
OVERCOMING OBSTACLES

AND BREAKING THROUGH BARRIERS

From cover to cover, the Bible highlights how obstacles, opposition and adversity are inevitable for those advancing God's sovereign agenda through entrepreneurial initiatives. Noah experienced scorn as he obeyed God's preposterous instructions to build an ark. Joseph endured betrayal, false accusations and over a decade of imprisonments before his prophetic destiny was realized. Even the Mighty Deliverer Moses encountered overwhelming lies, setbacks and hostile powers seeking to abort his world-changing assignment.

Throughout church history, those who have dared to live by God-inspired visions and build barrier-breaking enterprises for His glory have collided with fierce demonic resistance. From the Moravian missionaries whose entrepreneurial exploits funded the Great Awakening, to 21st century business leaders whose companies prioritize a Kingdom blueprint, the frontline soldiers advancing Heaven's economic strategies on earth have had to tenaciously persevere through intense opposition.

Make no mistake - if you're reading this book, you are a spiritual revolutionary in God's army of entrepreneurial Kingdom-influencers. Merely launching a business is not enough - you are giving birth to something that will shake nations, transform cultures and alter the course of human history as it accelerates the fulfillment of God's sovereign purposes. No wonder the powers of Hell are terrified and desperate to prevent it!

This chapter equips you with prophetic, war-counseling prayers that demolish opposition, obliterate obstacles and blast through all barriers from the pit of Hell. You will speak forth authoritative decrees that dismantle hindrances, confront attackers and access the authority that causes even the most formidable problem mountains to be cast into the sea. Get ready to break through!

Key Lessons

1. Resistance is Confirmation You're Doing Something Right - Don't be surprised by opposition and obstacles; they are confirmations your entrepreneurial vision is a legitimate threat to the Kingdom of Darkness.

2. Jesus Promised Us Authority Over Adversaries - At the cross, Jesus secured comprehensive legal authority for His

people to exercise dominion over adversaries and opposition through His Name.

3. Your Greatest Obstacles Are in the Spiritual Realm - Many barriers we face originate not in the physical realm, but through demonic interference in spiritual dimensions we cannot see.

4. Don't Rely Solely on Natural Solutions - Lasting breakthrough requires both practical action and authoritative prayer decrees that demolish unseen forces arrayed against you.

5. Offensive Prayers Enforce Victory - To overcome obstacles, you must shift from merely defensive prayers to enforcing offensive prayer strikes that command breakthrough.

UNCOMMON PRAYERS
Prayers.31-40

31. I demolish every obstacle, barrier, hindering spirit and assignment from Hell that has tried to prevent or delay the manifestation of the business vision and assignment You destined for me, O God.

32. I cancel the assignment of every spirit of delay, detour, distraction and blockade that has attempted to divert me from my course and postpone my breakthrough season of acceleration.

33. Exercising supreme authority over adversaries in Christ's name, I tear down demonic principalities and powers attempting to erect strongholds of delay, lack, opposition, resistance or setbacks over my life.

34. By the blood of the Lamb, I break generational curses of failure, lack, stagnation, and obstacles that have been passed down in my family line concerning business affairs.

35. I prophetically decree every mountain of opposition blocking the path to my promised future becomes a mere molehill as the high praises of God cause those mountains to be cast into the sea.

36. I cancel the assignment of blind guides and human counselors who with limited sight have hindered, discouraged or counseled stagnation and acceptance of obstacles impeding my progress.

37. I crush every principality and power resisting the advancement of God's Kingdom economic agenda & blueprint on

earth that this entrepreneurial vision is designed to accelerate.

38. I speak confusion into the camp of my spiritual adversaries attempting to create setbacks and detours, releasing angelic forces to chase them from their assignments.

39. I bind and silence every lying tongue and voice of discouragement attempting to abort this vision with words about its impossibility or feeding fear into my camp.

40. I prophesy supernatural ease and speed over every aspect of this entrepreneurial assignment, declaring by faith all obstruction must give way as God causes every crooked path to become straight before me.

CHAPTER 5
PROPHETIC PRAYERS TO SEIZE NEW OPPORTUNITIES

God's promise to Abraham wasn't just for innumerable descendants as the stars in the sky, but also for his seed to be so expansive that they would possess the metaphorical "gates" of influence, commerce and progression in cities around the world (Genesis 22:17). From the very foundations of covenantal blessing, God destined His people not just to exist, but to transition perpetually into new realms of territory, markets, enterprise and worldwide impact.

The Scriptures demonstrate a God who is always unveiling new spheres of promise and realms for His sons and daughters to possess. Under divine direction, Abraham's lineage migrated into new lands, Joseph was promoted to the new sphere of governing Egypt's economic affairs, and even the infant church of Acts penetrated new regions with astonishing speed through prophetic prayer and missionary thrusts into unreached territory.

Today, this same divine blueprint for advancement continues as Heaven reveals new business sectors for Kingdom innovation and economic spheres ready to be transformed by believers with entrepreneurial solutions. But seizing new territory doesn't happen automatically - it requires focused and prophetic prayers to tear open corridors and pathways that confront spiritual resistance attempting to restrict expansion.

The Holy Spirit prayers in this chapter will activate revelation concerning fresh opportunities lying in wait for you to possess. You will learn to pray with precision to seize that which God is trying to birth in the spirit realm concerning your business's reach into unreached regions, markets and mandates. Remember - revelation always precedes possession. So, get ready to aim, prophesy and capture new territory through these powerful petitions!

Key Lessons

1. There Are Always More Horizons God Wants You to Conquer - Although you may feel overwhelmed with your current load, God wants to continually transition you into new realms to steward.

2. When God Shows You Something New, It's now Yours to Possess - Every prophetic glimpse from Heaven carries divine authorization for you to activate it in the natural. Don't just spectate - take it!

3. Strategic Prophetic Prayers Enforce Your Possession - Seizing new territories and opportunities requires militant, spiritual enforcement prayers that cancel resistance and open gateways.

4. Walk Circumspectly for Fear of Missing Your Kairos Moments - Stay vigilant to perceive and seize prophetic windows when God orchestrates world events for divine shift and possessing new realms.

5. Every New Realm Impacts Kingdom Dominion on Earth - Expanding into new economic mountains positions you to be a change agent, influencing communities and cultures for righteousness.

UNCOMMON PRAYERS
Prayers.41-50

41. I activate prophetic discernment to have panoramic revelation of reservoirs of uncontested markets and territories You have reserved for me to possess in this new season, O God.

42. I lose the anointing of the Seer to receive detailed visions and divine intelligence concerning Kingdom opportunities and spheres reserved for my business to expand into.

43. As a wise master builder operating with blueprint revelation, I declare no human force can restrict or hinder my continual progression into new realms You have destined for me, Father.

44. I lose a baptism of courageous faith like the spies Caleb and Joshua, who saw conquered lands not as obstacles, but as

promised possessions for advancing God's agenda on earth.

45. By the covenant blood of Jesus, I uproot every spiritual force attempting to resist or impede my expansion into new regions, sectors, industries and harvest fields marked for me to possess.

46. I dispatch angelic reinforcements as departing angels tasked with assisting my ability to recognize and seize divinely orchestrated windows of opportunity for Kingdom-domain advancement.

47. I command the spiritual gateways and entry points into identified new territories and mandates to come off their hinges and open wide, allowing unobstructed access for advancement.

48. I prophetically recruit co-laborers and strategic partners currently dispersed in diverse locations to now align with this new vision and opportunity for economic Kingdom impact.

49. I speak confusion into the camp of demonic counselors & advisors feeding me the delusion of staying stuck and passive, rather than seizing the prophetic now.

50. From this point, I establish a militancy of vigilance to aggressively recognize and capitalize on every open window, divine appointment, and Kairos opportunity Heaven arranges.

CHAPTER 6

BIRTHING NEW IDEAS AND INNOVATIONS

Fostering an environment conducive to giving birth to new ideas and innovations was embedded into God's original blueprint for humanities' dominion assignment on the earth. After forming the first entrepreneurs, Adam and Eve, God emphasized that they were to "subdue" the earth through cultivating its fertile potential into productive bounty (Genesis 1:28). This divine directive carried profound prophetic implications concerning humanity's mandate to solve problems, maximize efficiency, and deliver excellence through ingenuity and continual process improvements.

All throughout Scripture, we witness ordinary people experiencing supernatural anointings of creativity and innovation to accomplish extraordinary assignments. From the skilled artisans and craftsmen who constructed the ornate details of Moses' wilderness Tabernacle, to the warrior-strategists like Nehemiah who birthed unprecedented building projects, the divine impartation of new ideas catapulted people into realms of influence.

God's heart hasn't changed. Just as He supernaturally endowed Spirit-led innovators throughout the Bible, He longs to impregnate modern-day entrepreneurs with childbirth visions that will transform industries and leave a legacy of solutions that outlive us. Like the biblical midwives in Exodus, it's time to prophetically speak to the spiritual wombs carrying kingdom-ideas and call forth conception, gestation and birthing of all God wants to release through you!

The womb-travailing, prophetic prayers in this chapter activate childbirth anointings and supernatural ideas that will solve complex challenges. Allow these declarations to act as spiritual doulas, equipping and empowering you to birth and nurture visions from Heaven with excellence. Get ready to blast through obstacles, accelerate progress and unleash innovations that rapidly make the status quo obsolete!

Key Lessons
1. The First Entrepreneurial Calling Was Innovation - Within the Genesis dominion mandate lies God's heart for His people to cultivate creation's potential through problem-solving ingenuity.

2. Every Entrepreneurial Idea Is First Conceived in the Spirit - Before any great innovation manifests on the earth, it's first conceived as a seed-thought that germinates in someone's spiritual womb through supernatural dream, vision or prompting.

3. Revelation Always Precedes Innovation - Major innovations and solutions require Spirit-birthed revelation and inspiration from Heaven to solve complex human problems in creative ways.

4. You Cannot Birth What You Do Not First Conceive - Just as in the natural, before a vision or new idea can be delivered, it must be conceived and carried through intentional spiritual "pregnancy."

5. Birth Through Prophetic Decrees and Declarations - From the birth canal of your mouth, you must prophetically travail through focused prayer decrees to facilitate the delivery of God-inspired ideas you've conceived.

UNCOMMON PRAYERS
Prayers.51-60

51. Activating a supernatural anointing for divine inspiration and continual overflow of innovative ideas that leave the world in awe of Your ingenuity, O God.

52. I prophetically call forth the manifestation of dreams and visions you have conceived within my spiritual womb concerning solutions, concepts and innovations that redefine excellence.

53. From the womb of Heaven's treasury of ideas, I call forth new revelations for products, services and business models that transform industries and radically disrupt the status quo.

54. I receive the spiritual mantle of master builders like Nehemiah and craftsmen who constructed the Tabernacle - those anointed to usher in innovations that facilitate Kingdom expansion.

55. I cancel the assignment of demonic principalities that have erected hindrances, obstacles and interference to prevent God-ordained ideas from manifesting on the earth.

56. I bind cycles of stagnation and a poverty spirit that positions me to merely maintain or replicate existing norms rather than pioneering new prototypes that upgrade the entire conversation.

57. Applying the blood covenant over the innovative ideas I birth, I declare no spirit of leakage, theft or another entity profiting

from or hijacking these revelations intended for my stewardship.

58. Any demonic obstruction erected in the spiritual realm to constrict or constrain divine inspiration is crushed, demolished and rendered powerless to hinder my progressive thinking.

59. I prophetically abort every premature attempt to miscarry or shoot down creative ideas from coming to full conception and manifestation in the physical universe.

60. I establish prayer-cover and activate angelic reinforcements from Heaven to nurture, protect, and accelerate the delivery process of spirit-conceived ideas until they take visible form on the earth.

CHAPTER 7
SPEAKING PROSPERITY AND ABUNDANCE INTO EXISTENCE

As you read through the Bible, it becomes evident that God's people were never intended to survive in perpetual lack, poverty, insufficiency or meager provisions. From the very onset of creation, when God fashioned the universe and all it contains purely by decreeing it into existence with His mouth, He instilled the embryonic blueprint for abundant prosperity through the power of the spoken word.

God's first recorded words to humanity model the divine template for actualizing abundance: "Be fruitful, multiply, fill the earth, and subdue it" (Genesis 1:28). These declarative blessings conveyed rich promises of lavish overflow, prolific reproduction and exercising dominion over a vast inheritance teeming with limitless resources and potential prosperity. Adam and Eve were commissioned to create an atmosphere pregnant with abundance by speaking forth God's kingdom reality over the earth.

This divine pattern continued as the Lord pronounced blessings of prosperity upon Noah and Abraham, while warning the latter, "I will make you a great nation, and I will bless you, and make your name great; and you shall be a blessing" (Genesis 12:2). As they boldly declared God's Word, impossibilities like barrenness, famine and lack melted away as Heaven's realities of abundance forcibly overtook circumstances in the physical realm.

Today, this template remains in force. The degree to which you accurately decree God's revelations from His Word, will determine the degree of supernatural abundance that manifests in your business affairs. The potent declarations and prophetic prayers in this chapter activate a portal for Kingdom wealth transference into your realm of industry and enterprise. Get ready to prophetically call forth biblical patterns of increase!

Key Lessons
1. We Are Created in the Image of a Prosperous God - Abundance should be your regular spiritual atmosphere and lifestyle, not the exception. Lack and scarcity were never His intent.

2. Blessings and Abundance Are Activated by Decree - God's blessings and supernatural flow of abundance are

appropriated by accurately declaring their existence into earthly reality.

3. Negative Circumstances Don't Define Your True Inheritance - Whether facing barrenness like Sarah or famine like Joseph, God's Word trumps your circumstances when spoken audaciously.

4. Jesus Secured the Wealth of the Wicked for Us - At the cross, Jesus awarded His people claim to confiscated abundance and previously hoarded by the Kingdom of Darkness and its human officials.

5. We Are Conduits of Limitless Supply - Every born-again believer has a spiritual umbilical cord connected to reams upon reams of heavenly storehouses of surplus blessing and prosperity.

UNCOMMON PRAYERS
Prayers.61-70

61. In communion with God's original spoken decree for humanity to experience abundance, I boldly declare the promise of overflow prosperity manifesting within my business affairs.

62. I prophetically announce the supernatural reversal of cycles of lack and scarcity by decreeing the heavenly reality of surplus provision and overflow supplying all that I require and more.

63. Just as with Abraham and Sarah, I contradict the facts of lack, barrenness and insufficiency through authoritative decrees

that command into existence like when God spoke creation into being.

64. I decree any past circumstances of lack and delay constricting manifestations of abundance and wealth to be demolished by the explosive power of prophetic decree activating overflow.

65. As a victor through Christ's finished work, I spoil principalities and powers by decreeing the wealth accumulated by the Kingdom of Darkness is now mine to steward for Kingdom perpetuation.

66. I activate the heavenly supply line of provision flowing to the earth by prophetically decreeing gateways and spiritual portals over my business to open, allowing resources from God's storehouses to deluge my circumstances.

67. By faith decree, I contradict negative confessions and unbelief that have prevented prosperity from being conceived and birthed, thereby releasing my inheritance of abundance.

68. I lose the supernatural mantle upon Abraham to prosper and release generational wealth regardless of adversities like famine, promising him a new tomorrow where the prevailing circumstances no longer dictate his future.

69. I decree the removal of any demonic gatekeepers restricting access to abundance through spoken commands that shatter hindrances and con

70. As a victor through Christ's finished work, I spoil principalities and powers by decreeing the wealth accumulated by the Kingdom of Darkness is now mine to steward for Kingdom perpetuation

CHAPTER 8
ATTRACTING AN OVERFLOW OF CLIENTS AND CUSTOMERS

From the very foundations of covenantal blessing in Genesis, God designed His people to experience perpetual cycles of abundance and overflow in whatever they set their hands to accomplish. When commissioning humanity with dominion over the earth, God pronounced the inaugural entrepreneurial charter and marketing strategy: "Be fruitful, multiply, fill the earth, and subdue it" (Genesis 1:28). This divine directive conveyed promises of prolific reproduction, exponential expansion and perpetual momentum.

Throughout Scripture, we witness this pattern of abundant overflow manifest in the lives of patriarchs. Despite periods of famine, lack and opposition, their bold confessions and obedient actions unlocked perpetual inflows of provision and rapidly expanding clientele with no lack of buyers (Proverbs 31:24). Entrepreneur-kings like David inherited abundance and saw their later years eclipse their beginnings as favor caused their spheres of influence to grow immensely.

In the New Testament, we see Jesus demonstrate Heaven's archetypal model for organically attracting massive crowds through a spiritual gravitational pull of teaching, healing and deliverance. He would go to remote places to be alone, yet multitudes continued flocking to Him

(Mark 1:45). What was the secret that drew such overwhelming demand?

It was the anointing and magnetic favor! Likewise for any entrepreneur - when you remain faithfully centered on your Kingdom essence, implementing Christ's heavenly business principles, you will cultivate irresistible appeal that continuously draws hungry crowds desiring what you carry.

This chapter will equip you to activate this same spirit of overflow allure through prophetic declarations and focused prayers. Get ready to witness the floodgates open as the favor of the Lord upon your business enterprise causes endless waves of clients to stream in, eclipsing what you ever imagined possible!

Key Lessons:
1. The Original Marketing Plan Was Favor-Driven Overflow - From Genesis onward, God has designed us to experience continual inflow of supply, opportunity and people.

2. Shortage Mentality Insults God's Intent for Your Business - Having just enough clients trickles in, plaguing entrepreneurs with scarcity fears. God wants to overwhelm you with abundance!

3. Attract Multitudes Through Heavenly Essences - Don't market by gimmicks, but

exude an irresistible anointing, making customers flock to what you truly carry within.

4. Abundance and Overflow Validate Your Obedience - When you faithfully serve Kingdom directives, abundance will chase and overtake you as a tangible sign you've stayed on-course.

5. Christ is the Model of Sustained Momentum - Jesus exemplified how to create perpetual overflow draw by staying centered on core apostolic essence and authority - not hype.

UNCOMMON PRAYERS
Prayers.71-80

71. I prophetically announce the opening of divine reservoirs of overflow from Heaven, summoning wave after wave of clients and customers to supernaturally flood my business.

72. I activate the multiplication anointing, decreeing exponential rates of expansion saturating my clientele and customer base - replicating like rapidly splitting cells!

73. I speak to the spiritual DNA of stagnation and customer defection, prophetically recalibrating the atomic structure to align with Heaven's divine growth pattern for continual addition.

74. By faith decree, I accelerate the momentum of favor causing multiplicative chain-reactions of overflow abundance to overtake my business in sales and customer acquisition.

75. I bind the spirits of shortage mentality, overactive attrition and drivelency causing customers to preemptively depart, cutting off their flow to feed this company vision.

76. I lose the boldness to decree blessing upon blessing overflowing from the throne of my King, drawing those famished for manifestations of Kingdom prosperity to my doors.

77. I call forth the overwhelming displays of miracle provision witnessed in biblical figures like Joseph, attracting multitudes desperate for help through divinely orchestrated opportunities.

78. Through declarations of overflow, I position this enterprise as God's lighthouse beacon attracting all ships in the stormy seas surrounding us desperate for our services.

79. Any generational curses or demonic legislations prophesied against my bloodline or this company from experiencing abundant overflow and overflow of clients are shattered now in Jesus' Name!

80. I recruit the service of angels bearing the ministry of overwhelming overflow to

amplify Heaven's thunderous summons over this region causing multitudes to run to our sound.

CHAPTER 9
SUPERNATURAL WISDOM FOR STRATEGIC DECISION-MAKING

Throughout the biblical narrative, God has imparted the premium currency of supernatural wisdom to Spirit-led entrepreneurs and business leaders to make flawless strategic decisions. When God made covenant with Abraham, the father of faith received divine wisdom to amass immense wealth through agricultural innovations and strategic property acquisitions across vast regions.

The wisdom of Joseph secured favor with Pharaoh, promoted him to essentially become prime minister over Egypt's entire economic engine, and implement brilliant strategies that not only saved multitudes from famine, but allowed him to acquire all of Egypt's wealth.

In the New Testament, the apostles operated with profound wisdom and divine strategies that propelled the exponential expansion of the early church across cultural barriers with stunning efficiency. Paul alone was able to plant congregations throughout the Roman empire within a mere decade, funded by entrepreneurial tent-making ventures along his journeys.

Today, pioneering business leaders who prioritize biblical meditation and humble pursuit of Heaven's wisdom continue to experience supernatural insight, seeing puzzles with clarity no study or statistical analysis could achieve. From receiving guidance for product pivots to prophetic intelligence on mergers or market fluctuations years ahead, those who make decisions in sync with Heaven's wisdom prosper while those solely informed by earthly knowledge flounder.

The revelatory prayers in this chapter activate portals for God's wisdom to transcend your natural mind and impart profitable solutions. No longer will you succumb to fear, conventional thinking, hasty decisions or ignorance that leave money on the table. Instead, these petitions unleash the same wisdom from above that produces mathematical genius, scientific breakthroughs and entrepreneurial innovations that make a transformational global impact. Get ready to discover the vantage point from which all of Heaven's resources are available!

Key Lessons:
1. Wisdom Is the Supreme Asset for Leaders Wisdom trumps all other pursuits, being the principal force-multiplier to expand businesses far beyond natural limitations.

2. God Generously Imparts His Wisdom to the Humble - Those who approach God with humility and hunger, He can entrust with strategies typically reserved for kings.

3. Heaven's Wisdom Solves Impossible Scenarios - When we encounter complex issues our faculties cannot untangle, God's wisdom slices through with practical genius no algorithm could match.

4. Wisdom Unlocks Timing and Precision - Many breakthroughs occur when we receive wisdom to act with impeccable precision at the divinely appointed nanosecond determined by Heaven's calendar.

5. Prayer Activates Revelatory Wisdom Downloads - While meditation can certainly impart wisdom incrementally, focused prayer is the catalyst for instantaneous downloads of time-condensed revelation.

UNCOMMON PRAYERS
Prayers.81-90

81. I forsake all reliance on finite human wisdom, choosing daily to receive unlimited wisdom from You, God, making my path blazing with light upon light!

82. I break the assignment of demonic forces that have worked to cloud my

judgement, impart confusion, or veil paths of wisdom reserved for me in Christ.

83. I plead Your covenant promises to lavish wisdom on the humble and those who ask in faith, releasing torrents of supernatural solutions into my mind.

84. Like Solomon and Daniel, I call forth the spirit of excellence in wisdom that positions me to effortlessly unravel mysteries and impossible conundrums no natural study could resolve.

85. I decree any past regrettable, costly decisions resulting from lacking celestial wisdom are retroactively resolved and course-corrected by new disclosures now!

86. I prophetically recruit legions of godly advisors and counselors with the mind of Christ to partner with the wisdom

downloads I steward from Heaven's courtrooms.

87. I lose the mantle for wisdom in administration, management and government just as Joseph received to structure organizations and systems efficiently.

88. Any present strategic decisions paralyzed by ignorance; I provide clarity now by commanding the revelatory lightbulb of wisdom to illuminate all blind spots!

89. I call forth divine accelerators of wisdom, equipping me to receive in moments revelatory insights typically reserved for years of tedious study.

90. I establish prayer-covered environments of angelic assistance where legions from the Wisdom Realm can surround me imparting God's applied knowledge

CHAPTER 10
BUILDING A KINGDOM-MINDED COMPANY CULTURE

From the earliest chapters of Genesis, God embedded prophetic patterns concerning His intention for companies and organizations to operate with Kingdom-minded values at their core.

When fashioning humanity, God established a theocratic chain-of-command placing King Jesus as the preeminent Head over all rule and authority (Colossians 2:10). Adam and Eve were commissioned as vice-regents, or "CEOs," under His sovereign headship to steward dominion over earth's vast resources and potential in worshipful obedience.

This divine precedent continued as God raised up Spirit-led entrepreneurs like Joseph, Daniel, and Nehemiah who prioritized implementing Heaven's leadership values within the organizations they governed. Despite representing a marginal minority voice amidst polytheistic cultures, these administrators enforced policies and working environments that facilitated holistic flourishing in alignment with God's Kingdom blueprint.

In the New Testament, Jesus provided the Master-Class in spiritual organizational culture by developing twelve faithful understudies who would serve as prototypes to usher in the church - God's worldwide Kingdom enterprise on the earth. Over a three-year internship, Jesus modeled what it meant to build a healthy, supernaturally-potent team atmosphere rooted in authentic discipleship.

Today's pioneering business and organizational leaders are awakening to the reality that merely attaining profit objectives is insufficient; true success demands championing Heaven's comprehensive definition of prosperity and dedicating resources to bring God's order and justice to earthly affairs. Developing a company ethos informed by Kingdom priorities - like modeling generosity, mutual honor, ethical practices and compassion for the marginalized - has become the sustainable path forward.

The prayers in this chapter activate wisdom for establishing your organizational culture as a microcosm of Heaven's dominion - a sacred embassy releasing righteousness throughout the spheres you influence. Through them, you will override misaligned practices while encoding your entire enterprise with divine DNA that breathes the Lord's Presence and advances outposts for His sovereignty to be established over every arena of human endeavor.

Key Lessons
1. Your Organization Is an Embassy of Heaven on Earth - Whatever you steward has been commissioned as a vehicle to expand the Kingdom's values and priorities into every sphere of influence.

2. Organizational Health Transcends Material Profit - A company that pursues anything less than biblical shalom prosperity - the integrated flourishing of every stakeholder's spiritual, emotional and relational well-being - is unsustainable.

3. Kingdom Companies Model Heaven's Order - The values embedded in your organizational culture should provide a visible, functioning sample of how things operate when Heaven fully governs.

4. Kingdom Companies Awaken to Disciple Nations - Beyond just making money, you have a mandate to leverage your company's influence to transform communities and mentor multitudes into righteousness.

5. Prayer Provides Organizational Covering - To sustain a Kingdom-minded culture, you must prioritize fervently praying,

declaring, and prophetically establishing Heaven's atmospheres and parameters throughout your operations.

UNCOMMON PRAYERS
Prayers.91-100

91. I decree a reformatting and recalibration of this company away from prioritizing profitability apart from purpose, to fully aligning with the Kingdom agenda of the Lord Jesus Christ.

92. I eradicate any vestige remaining of secular mindsets that relegate faith as

separate from organizational operations. I enforce Jesus as the true CEO over our vision and activities!

93. I demolish the anti-Christ spirit and its toxic byproducts of greed, exploitation, and ethical compromise that have permeated corporate cultures across society. Jesus is Lord here!

94. I prophetically recruit and mobilize mentors, forerunners, and exemplars who model Heaven's standards for leadership, equity, dignity, and holistic prosperity.

95. I bind the Deception of success metrics and "bottom line at all costs" mentalities that sacrifice people and virtue on the altar of materialism and institutional preservation.

96. I lose mantles of favor like Nehemiah and Daniel upon leaders in spheres to rebuild crumbling foundations while instituting values-driven cultures honoring to the Lord.

97. I reverse any dishonorable flow concerning employees, customers, and stakeholders - replacing it with Heaven's purposes to extend loving dignity to humans as image-bearers.

98. I prophetically weed out leaders/influencers within our ranks who refuse to uphold righteous character and instead use their leverage for ego-driven agendas.

99. I overthrow operating systems premised on hierarchical power and control, replacing them with biblical order that

equips the saints to fulfill their unique assignments in Christ.

100. I consecrate the spiritual environments throughout our operations with the purifying fire of the Holy Spirit so that only what has been birthed in Heaven can flourish within.

CHAPTER 11
PRAYING FOR EXCELLENCE AND PEAK PERFORMANCE

From start to finish, the Scriptures unveil God as the original Master of excellence - the consummate Creator whose every action manifested unsurpassable quality, beauty and perfection. When establishing a template for humanity's entrepreneurial mandate to cultivate creation's resources with dominion, God defined excellence as the benchmark: "Be fruitful, multiply, fill the earth, and subdue it" (Genesis 1:28). Meeting this mandate necessitated bringing Heaven's supernatural excellence into all human endeavors.

Study the lives of patriarchs like Joseph and Daniel - individuals who consistently modeled excellent performance at the highest levels possible. Undergirding their success was a vibrant devotional life of prayer, fasting, and attunement to God's wisdom, enabling them to outperform all their contemporaries and achieve mind-boggling accomplishments.

Jesus revealed the ultimate mastery of excellence in everything He set His hand to accomplish. From teaching to healing to evangelistic impact, the Lord Jesus performed everything with incomparable perfection, quality, and insuperable effect - leaving onlookers awestruck. Yet Jesus credited His excellent life to staying connected to the Source: "The Son can do nothing of Himself, but what He sees the Father do" (John 5:19).

Today, Christ's disciples seeking to maximize excellence and achieve pinnacle performance in their business operations or careers have discovered the secret to sustained success: developing an unbroken communion with the Father to receive His excellent strategies, wisdom and impartation continually. It's this intimacy with God that positions you for greatest fruitfulness.

The declarations in this chapter fight to demolish mental barriers, spiritual fatigue or bodily limitations as you wage spiritual warfare to excel. Pray these focused prayers to supercharge your energy, wisdom and favor for impact - making your outputs world-class every time! Get ready to walk in new realms of excellence as you boldly consecrate all your labors as an offering to the Highest God.

Key Lessons:
1. Excellence Is God's Divine Nature - As image-bearers of the Perfect Creator, excellence isn't an arbitrary goal, but the very essence of who we are called to become in Christ.

2. Excellent Performance Glorifies God - When we walk in Christ's victorious Presence, our conduct radiates supernatural excellence that declares God's reality to onlookers.

3. Intimacy Is the Engine of Excellent Outputs - Disciples achieve excellence not through self-effort, but by resting in continual union with Christ who flows divine strategies, wisdom and ability.

4. Excellence Requires Sacrifice and Holiness - Like high-performance athletes, maintaining peak levels of spiritual excellence demands a rigorous devotional lifestyle separated unto God.

5. Excellence Provokes Multiplication - When governed by excellence, your endeavors naturally draw favor, increase and exponential harvests beyond your individual capacity.

UNCOMMON PRAYERS
Prayers.101-110

101. I overthrow physical and mental fatigue or limitations attempting to hinder me

from walking in excellence by accessing the resurrection life of Christ within as my Source.

102. I demolish generational mindsets and ceilings that have tried to define excellence according to secular, average standards unworthy of my royal identity in Jesus.

103. I break assignments from the Kingdom of Darkness attempting to divert me from excellence through compromise, ethical shortcuts or lackluster apathy.

104. I uproot any spiritual force of Distraction seeking to hi-jack my attention or knock me out of flow-state while I'm focused on Spirit-inspired projects and outputs.

105. By the Blood of the Lamb, I cancel out all physical and mental weariness associated with past seasons of over-work and unhealthy striving outside the abiding Vine.

106. I reverse the curse of inconsistency that has allowed only sporadic excellent performance while carelessly drifting into patterns of mediocrity and missed windows.

107. I prophetically recruit and commission angelic reinforcements whose assignments are to empower and accelerate my pursuit of excellent endeavors honoring Christ.

108. I call forth the anointing and mantle of excellence modeled by our Lord Jesus Christ to rest upon my life now.

109. I break assignments from the Kingdom of Darkness attempting to divert me from excellence through compromise, ethical shortcuts or lackluster apathy

110. By the Blood of the Lamb, I cancel out all physical and mental weariness associated with past seasons of over-work and unhealthy striving outside the abiding Vine.

CHAPTER 12
DEFEATING THE SPIRIT

OF LACK AND LIMITATION

From the genesis of Scripture, lack and limitation were never God's intention for His entrepreneurs and Kingdom ambassadors on the earth. When fashioning the cosmos, God intentionally filled the universe with an overabundance of resources, raw materials and creative potential - more than enough for humanity to cultivate and multiply fruitfulness without restriction. Lack and scarcity were foreign concepts.

Yet almost immediately, lack tried to establish a footing through the serpent's deceptive narrative convincing Adam and Eve they didn't have enough. Despite being granted access to every tree's fruit save one, they were seduced into crazing after the lone forbidden object based on a poverty spirit's convincing lie there wasn't enough.

Throughout history, this same demonic spirit of lack and limitation has stalked God's children, peddling perceptions of inadequacy and insufficiency designed to sabotage dreams and throttle back prosperous destinies. From feeding cravings for more mere moments after miraculous manifestations of abundance, to spawning toxic mindsets content to just survive rather than thrive, lack poisons visions before they can materialize.

But the cross of Christ has disarmed these foul powers once and for all! While navigating wilderness testings and periods of temporary deficiency for refinement purposes, every believer has been awarded access to unlimited resource reservoirs situated in heavenly places. No shortage can ultimately hinder you when connected to Him who owns vast storehouses bulging with surplus supplies.

The warfare declarations in this chapter are your spiritual ammunition for aggressive combat against any assignment of lack or limitation over your endeavors. Use these militant prayers to demolish mental strongholds constricting your capacity to conceive abundance and exercise dominion. Get ready to overpower the enemy's credibility and prophesy perpetual overflow into existence!

Key Lessons

Lack Was Never the Original Design – God intentionally pre-stocked the earth's reservoirs with surplus resources and creative potential to sustain overflowing prosperity when we operate according to His patterns.

2. Lack Operates Primarily Through Deception - The primary weapon of lack is deceit aimed at hijacking your perceptions and expectations through poverty mindsets and limiting beliefs.

3. Abundance Flows from Divine Perspective - Once you perceive from your heavenly Father's vantage point of lavish surplus, impossibilities evaporate concerning supply and provision.

4. Deliverance Unlocks the Flow of Abundance - You cannot simultaneously embrace negative mindsets and

breakthrough to unlimited resources. Freedom is prerequisite to accessing overflow abundance.

5. Prophetic Decrees Override Visible Circumstances - Circumstances of lack cannot remain when you consistently prophesy the realities of Heaven where supply is unlimited and nothing is impossible.

UNCOMMON PRAYERS

Prayers.111-120

111. I forcefully renounce and demolish all deception, lies, and limiting mindsets rooted in the poverty spirit that have tried to hijack my perceptions concerning abundance.

112. I break generational curses, cycles and negative DNA patterns on both sides of my family line involving lack, perpetual struggle, deficiency and never having enough.

113. By forceful decree, I reverse all circumstances of lack and limitation over my business endeavors and release prophetic utterances shattering constricting cycles of inertia.

114. I bind the spirit of lack from operating in any form over my realm of influence and

business affairs. No scarcity pays allegiance to me any longer!

115. I prophetically call forth the supernatural intervention of God's turnaround angelic reinforcements to bombard obstacles and hindrances with surplus bombardment and overwhelming deliveries of abundance!

116. I speak to any dormant seeds, ideas or ventures that have stalled out due to scarcity of resources and prophetically call forth resurrection life to quicken growth and multiplication.

117. In forceful decrees, I spiritually legislate continuous economic increase, debt freedom, and financial overflow to become the new norm in my situation.

118. I prophetically decree I am forever dispersing and never lacking, replenishing and never emptying, with effortless channels of abundance continually flowing to me!

119. I demolish mental strongholds related to anxiety, fear or worry over supply lines being interrupted, commanding divine Providence to uphold me perpetually.

120. I cancel the assignment of dream killers and human counselors peddling limiting beliefs, lack mindsets or trying to impose ceilings over vision due to perceived limitations.

CHAPTER 13
PRAYERS FOR HARMONIOUS PARTNERSHIPS AND TEAMWORK

From the dawn of creation, God embedded blueprint patterns for synergistic partnership and harmonious teamwork into His ultimate entrepreneurial venture. When conceiving humanity, He didn't design Adam as a self-sufficient individual to dominate the earth in isolation, but rather to co-labor alongside a companion partner in Eve, for shadowing Christ's Bride operating as His join their (Genesis 2:18-24).

Throughout Scripture, we witness how God consistently deploys teams of partners to fulfill assignments requiring interdependent collaboration and covering one another's vulnerabilities. Whether Moses required Aaron's support, David needed Jonathan's covenant partnership, or Jesus commissioned the apostolic team of The Twelve, much of God's activity on earth has been accomplished through unified teams with interlinking anointings.

Likewise, the early church's exponential expansion across cultures happened at an accelerated rate because of synergistic co-laboring - from leadership couples like Priscilla and Aquila functioning as entrepreneurial church-planters, to the convergence of apostolic and prophetic anointings, to churches networked across regions providing supply lines for one another's prosperity.

In the modern era, Spirit-led entrepreneurs and leaders continue to experience supernatural increase through multiplied fruitfulness when their individual gifts synergize collaboratively within teams and partnerships that spiritually complement, not conflict with, one another's strengths.

The prophetic declarations in this chapter activate grace for attracting and cultivating redemptive synergy with other Christ-centered visionaries and difference-makers through unified operations. No longer will the enemy disrupt teamwork in your spheres of influence; these prayers invite Heaven's reinforcements to connect the required alliances and strategic alliances your endeavors require to maximize harvest. Synergy cubed is your portion!

Key Lessons

1. No Teams, No Destiny - From creation's opening scenes, team synergy was woven into Heaven's Kingdom blueprint for accomplishing Earth's dominion assignment.

2. One Gift Does Not Release God's Full Potential - Your individual graces require symbiotic connection with complementary gifts to maximize fruitfulness and release God's boundless solutions to complex challenges.

3. The Power of Alignment Births Revival - When Kingdom ambassadors synergize graces through divine orchestration rather than dissension, spiritual awakenings result as a magnified demonstration of Christ's glory and authority manifest.

4. Intentional Prayer Attracts Divine Connections - While some partnerships occur through natural relationships, many are spiritually arranged as you steward prophetic petitions to partner with those Heaven has prepared to work wondrously together.

5. Exercise Spiritual Authority Over Discord You cannot passively hope for synergy; you must aggressively enforce it by displacing forces of relational strife, competition or independent self-reliance.

UNCOMMON PRAYERS
Prayers.121-130

121. I establish an atmosphere of supernatural synergy and networking upon every sphere of my endeavors that necessitates the convergence of complementary gifts, anointings and resources.

122. I bind the anti-Christ spirit of disunity, competition, jealousy and relational strife from interfering with or sabotaging any covenanted alliance or divine connection undergirding my harvest assignments.

123. I speak charismatic favor over my capacity to attract and empower strategic relationships providentially tailored to cover my personal/organizational weaknesses with inherent strengths.

124. I prophetically recruit grace alliances and Kingdom entrepreneurial networks with symbiotic interdependence ordained to usher in rapid expansion and revival to my limited sphere of influence.

125. I cancel all past negative projections that accepted limiting myths promoting rugged individualism over collaborative synergy as the paradigm for maximum effectiveness.

126. Any discordant relationships operating from woundings, pride, or independent self-reliance, I declare a revival of mutual honor and Peter/John-like symbiotic unity where iron truly sharpens iron.

127. Over communities and spheres of influence I steward, I decree a spirit of

teamwork, sacrifice, and covenantal alignment to become the new prevailing spirit displacing me-first agendas.

128. I demolish all stubborn forces attempting to resist divine connection with overarching Revival Alliances and Kingdom Entrepreneurial Networks slated for next-level synergy.

129. I secure wisdom from Heaven on intentional communication and bonding rituals that preserve

130. I cancel all past negative projections that accepted limiting myths promoting rugged individualism over collaborative synergy as the paradigm for maximum effectiveness.

CHAPTER 14

BREAKING GENERATIONAL CURSES OF FAILURE

From Eden's opening scenes until today, generational iniquity and familial sins have compounded into dysfunctional cycles and self-perpetuating curses sabotaging subsequent generations from experiencing God's promised prosperity. The Bible records how Yahweh Himself establishes this sobering principle: "For I, the Lord your God, am a jealous God, visiting the iniquity of the fathers upon the children to the third and fourth generations" (Exodus 20:5).

Generational patterns like poverty, failed businesses, divorce, abuse and mental/emotional torment don't materialize by chance - they are spiritually conceived and "birthed" through anatomies of sin awaiting renewal through deliverance. When unchecked, destructive cycles reinforce themselves like compounding interest until families remain bound in a complex of limiting mindsets, self-sabotage and demonic legal rights.

Thankfully, Jesus demolished Hell's grip on perpetuating failure by canceling out all Adamic sin and ancestral iniquity through His redemptive work! Where repeat dysfunctions once dogged families with growing intensity, the cross has legally disarmed their power over those who denounce them by faith and actively sever covenants with failure's synergistic accumulation.

This chapter will equip you to prophetically uproot and demolish any generational curses of failure, stagnation, lack or limitation that have tried ensnaring your family lineage. No longer will you remain shackled to past norms or capped by prior belief system "DNA" constraining you from experiencing unqualified breakthrough! These authoritative prayers lose you into new realms of possibility where you permanently override cycles of mediocrity to step into your overcoming inheritance.

Key Lessons
1. Failure Breeds More Failure by Default - Like any living organism, curses of failure feed upon their own perpetuation with compounding force across subsequent generations until broken.

2. You Cannot Flourish Beyond Your Belief Systems - Breaking out of mediocrity mandates audacious renunciations of any limiting mindsets or agreements with failure's legitimacy over your life.

3. Repentance Precedes Family Restoration - Prior to commanding breakthrough over generational patterns, ownership of iniquities must occur to revoke Satan's legal rights.

4. Decrees Override Spiritual DNA Code - Just as Jesus disarmed Adamic sin's power through His authoritative blood covenant, your proclamations uproot destructive familial DNA.

5. Families Pass Inheritance Not Only of Wealth but Wisdom - Once liberated from the poverty spirit, your children now receive upgraded familial DNA of prosperity wisdom.

UNCOMMON PRAYERS
Prayers.131-140

131. By the authority in Christ's name, I permanently renounce and demolish all generational iniquities and historical covenants with failure from both my paternal and maternal bloodlines.

132. In forceful repentance, I revoke all legal rights allowing demonic forces and cycles of lack, stagnation, bankruptcy, or self-sabotage to negatively affect my affairs.

133. I prophetically override negative family narratives and belief systems rooted in curse patterns of mediocrity that have hijacked the spiritual DNA of success.

134. I break all generational bondages of addiction, abuse, mental/emotional

torment, or oppression operating through epigenetics or familiar spirit agency. Enough is enough!

135. I cancel out all demonic verdicts and prophetic words of doom spoken over previous generations that have continued echoing limiting resonance today. Truth overrides curses!

136. By faith, I reclaim my birthright and extract my inheritance portion from all wealth, wisdom and heavenly resources meant to empower me as a world-shaper and pacesetter for righteousness.

137. I pull down strongholds of dishonor and disrespect intergenerationally transferred that have fostered low self-worth, undermining my sense of Kingdom entitlement and blessing.

138. I decree restoration and resurrection over any families, businesses or initiatives that have endured miscarriage, failure or premature flatlining in previous generations.

139. I lose mantles for prosperity like Joseph, who though deeply betrayed never lost his generational inheritance despite coming from a troubled lineage of family dysfunction.

140. I prophetically steward resurrection life for my family line, commanding blessings, covenants, destinies and inheritances of success previously aborted or remaining unrealized to break forth in new manifestations of glory!

CHAPTER 15

COMMANDING DOORS TO OPEN INTERNATIONALLY

From the book of Genesis onward, the Scriptures blaze with God's sovereign intentionality for His Covenant People to exercise dominion across every nation under heaven. Through covenants with patriarchs like Abraham and Joseph, we see Heaven's pattern of strategically deploying His influence across cultural borders and regions to extend His Kingdom rule.

Later chronicles record the advance of God's Kingdom physically manifesting as Heaven's representatives entered into unreached realms and territories. From Moses leading Israel through enemy strongholds into new lands, to the Apostles ushering in unprecedented globalization of Christ's ecclesia after the outpouring in

Acts, Scripture displays God's heart for borders, obstacles and resistance to part like the Red Sea as barriers dissolve before His mighty armies.

In this crucial era of history, the final frontiers for world evangelization and societal transformation are opening before pioneering business leaders and entrepreneurs who prioritize discipling nations and shifting cultures over mere financial objectives. As these Kingdom revolutionaries steward prophetic petitions and decrees, they are witnessing swift acceleration into realms of global impact.

In this chapter, the declarations contained within its pages activate divine checkmate sequences demolishing demonic obstruction and wrestling open international gateways for new zones of influence to manifest. Through them, you will speak forth unprecedented favor, relocation of resources, migrations of peoples, and financial increase rushing into your operations.

Get ready to supercharge your global sphere of impact as these authoritative prayers access Heaven's strategies and timetables for rapid expansion. Where previous generations toiled with minimal ground taken, you will decree swift advancement and sovereignty over once fortified, hostile territories becoming seasons of harvest!

Key Lessons

1. The Earth Is Reserved as God's Inheritance God has destined the nations and their resources for reconstituting the worldwide rule of Christ's Kingdom at His return.

2. Expansion Is Not Optional but Biblical Mandate - From Adam to the Apostles, Christ-followers were commissioned to advance strategically across new realms and regions through colonizing influence until He returns.

3. God Remains Undeterred by Resistance - No satanic opposition, cultural obstructions or hostile forces can ultimately resist Heaven's advance as you enforce expansion through authoritative faith.

4. Speedy Acceleration Is Prophetically Spoken into Existence - Jesus compressed

centuries of gradual advancement into just decades as Apostolic teams decreed supernatural favor and breakthrough expansion.

5. The Great Commission is Married to Great Wealth Transfer - As Gospel penetration increases, creator insights and resources follow, further empowering society's transformation.

UNCOMMON PRAYERS

Prayers.141-150

141. As a mighty Warrior for Christ's Kingdom, I command the spiritual gateways of access over new international spheres of influence to fling wide open now like floodgates and border crossings welcoming an invasion of light!

142. By the blood covenant, I demolish the anti-Christ infrastructure of resistance that has attempted to obstruct, oppose and erect strongholds impeding swift geographical expansion into nations reserved for discipleship.

143. I dispatch angelic convoys of territoriality breakthrough to precede and eject hostile spiritual forces squatting over coveted regions targeted for establishing Christ's dominion.

144. I prophetically accelerate the convergence of divine connections, economic alliances, attunements of timing and confluences of people migration funneling the favor dynamics required for next-level globalization.

145. From the courts of Heaven, I loose and engage the full accompaniment of breakthrough angelic hosts assigned to support rapid global advancement - overcoming resistance to establish international revival hubs where none previously existed!

146. I pull down all satanic thrones of cultural resistance to Christianity's infiltration and establish Jesus as preeminent King over every ethnic worldview enslaved by false religion!

147. I permanently revoke all hindrances impeding financial blessing from rushing into these new spheres as Kingdom economic engines manifesting resources to fund transformation on the ground!

148. By authoritative decree, I call forth the opening of double-portion Grace doors in previously anti-Christian regions where miraculous sign-wonders validate Christ's authority over all spiritual opposition!

149. I engage a mother lode of favor manifestations including swift removals of anti-Kingdom regimes and establishments of ruling officials labeled gatekeepers and advocates for societal blessing.

CHAPTER 16

UNSTOPPABLE PRAYERS FOR INFLUENCE AND IMPACT

From the very foundations of the biblical narrative, God has worked through human influencers and cultural change-agents to extend His sovereign rule over every sphere of society. Whether it was entrepreneurial patriarchs like Abraham and Joseph who amassed great wealth and power, or kingdom officials like Joseph and Daniel strategically placed within hostile regimes, Heaven has always prioritized positioning those labeled "Josephs" to reshape societal directives and structures.

When studying the life of Christ, we find the ultimate case study in achieving global, multi-generational influence from seemingly humble beginnings. Though born to an outcast family in a remote colony, Jesus' short three-year public ministry sparked a tectonic civilizational disruption - catalyzing a philosophical revolution with ripple effects that impacted everything from ethics and science to government and economics worldwide.

Just as an atomic bomb's shockwave releases inconceivable energy from a tiny source, the explosive power behind Jesus' life detonated through a small band of devoted followers who decreed His influence with unstoppable audacity after Pentecost. Within one generation, this Spirit-fueled movement infiltrated Roman society at every level - from the Caesars' palace to the professional trade guilds - igniting societal transformations that still reverberate today.

In our modern era, the social diffusion of Christianity's influence faces increasing resistance through Cancel Culture, censorship of biblical values, corporate compromises and government overreach opposing the Gospel's advancement. Yet a new breed of entrepreneurs and industry leaders are arising - emboldened reformers who have discovered the transformative power of cultivating cultures of audacious, unstoppable prayer for societal renaissance.

The Holy Spirit-inspired petitions in this chapter activate greater measures of influence and impact than social engineers or elite machinations can produce. Through them, you will speak revival wildfire into cultural mountains while smashing demonic agendas entrenched by dark powers within society's power corridors. Get ready to experience first-hand how one God-inspired decree can trigger societal earthquakes that dismantle anti-Christ fortresses in a single brushstroke!

Key Lessons:

1. Influence is Achieved Through Spiritual Strategies - Worldly systems can only provide limited impact before running out of momentum. Accessing Heaven's resources multiplies your societal imprint.

2. Culture Shapes Reality More Than Politics Don't obsess over mere politics or power structures. Those who shape belief systems and philosophies redirecting culture are the real change agents.

3. Sustained Impact Requires Continual Reformation - One revival cycles into the next season of resistance, necessitating courage to keep decreeing positive upgrades without compromise.

4. Persevere Like the Apostles - From prison cells to the throne room, early Christ followers never retreated or accepted being sidelined from decreeing Kingdom influence over civilizations.

5. Babylon's Fall Makes Room for Zion's Increase - Anti-Christ agendas create temporary chaos and instability but also clearing space for resurrection of Christ's influence through Kingdom ambassadors.

UNCOMMON PRAYERS
Prayers.151-160

151. I expose the matrix of anti-Christ agendas eroding foundations of society and dismantling this ungodly infrastructure of indoctrination, legislation, and unrighteous activism.

152. I release battering rams of breakthrough into cancel culture's stranglehold restricting the influence of biblical values in public arenas of society.

153. I prophetically cancel laws and ordinances hostile to the Gospel's advancement, decreeing favor increasing like a flood bringing policies into Kingdom-alignment.

154. I demolish interdimensional portals where demonic strongmen project unrighteous mindsets deceiving societies into systemic wickedness taking root.

155. I prophetically recruit generations of young revolutionaries burning with holy zeal and courage to decree biblical renaissance into colleges and educational spheres.

156. Over industries and professional guilds, I release refreshing for culture-shaping influencers and creatives to fearlessly produce works expressing kingdom realities.

157. I pull down illegitimate anti-Christ thrones actively occupying power positions throughout society's governing systems and media outlets.

158. I seal in revival breakthroughs already underway spreading to every environment: neighborhoods awakened, cities transformed, ministries unleashed!

159. Where Hell has attempted to legislate society's descent into darkness, I decree spiritual resurrection over those desolate arenas groaning for rebirth.

160. By the Spirit's resurrection power, I prophesy resurrection life over any Christ-honoring movement or righteous cause that's grown cold or ineffective.

CHAPTER 17
PLEADING THE BLOOD FOR PROTECTION AND SECURITY

From the earliest scenes in Scripture, the shedding of innocent blood has been a sacred act establishing covenantal protection and spiritual security. When instituting the Passover in Exodus, God required each Israelite household to slaughter an unblemished lamb and smear its blood upon the doorposts and lintels as a seal of divine security. This fearsome act activated the preserving power of the shed blood, causing the destroying angel to literally "pass over" any dwelling under the covenant's coverage.

Throughout the Old Testament, blood covenants and sacrificial systems laid redemptive foundations highlighting how the ultimate sacrifice of God's spotless Lamb would one day establish an eternally binding covenant guaranteeing security, preservation and complete shalom for all who took shelter beneath it.

At the cross, Jesus' tortuous death culminated in His precious blood being poured out - an immortal life essence containing resurrection power, victory over sin and death, and authority to demolish every stronghold of the enemy. Like impenetrable bug repellent, the blood causes demonic powers to recoil with terror from those covered under Heaven's covenant.

In our modern era, pleading the full work of Christ's blood through authoritative prayers actually releases tangible measures of spiritual security and divine protection over

God's redeemed people. Just as the Israelites found preservation inside homes marked by blood's seal during the plagues of Egypt, businesses, properties, investments, entrepreneurial endeavors and territories claimed by the blood become fortresses largely inaccessible to demonic sabotage.

The focused prayers comprising this chapter activate blood covenant promises, strategically pleading the full work of Christ's atonement as an impenetrable fortress spanning every sphere of your life and enterprise. You will establish blood lines that cannot be violated, erect hedge protections and loose divine angelic guardians - to secure your realms from territorial spirits, soul hunters and wickedness in high places. Get ready to find perfect peace as you learn to apply the blood to every situation!

Key Lessons

1. The Blood Is God's Supreme Covenant Seal - Like Passover, Christ's blood establishes a new unbreakable covenant ultimately preserving those covered from destruction.

2. Pleading the Blood Releases Resurrection Power - Within the blood's sacred flow courses Christ's authority over death, sin, and all opposing works of darkness.

3. Blood Covenants Establish Divine Asylum The spiritual territories and boundaries covered by Christ's blood comprise zones of refugee status from Satan's jurisdictions.

4. Assign Words to the Blood for Full Effect - Like applying the blood marker on the Israelites' doors, we activate the blood covenant by intentionally declaring and assigning its authority.

5. The Blood Spiritually Positions You for Victory - Pleading the blood's protection inoculates you from Lucifer's accusations and establishes setting for prevailing dominantly.

UNCOMMON PRAYERS
Prayers.161-170

161. I reverently and gratefully proclaim the precious blood of Jesus Christ and all its covenant promises over every sphere of my life, business and spheres of influence.

162. I plead the blood over my mind to demolish cycles of torment, fear, and oppression - renewing my thought life by the blood's resurrection power!

163. I assign the blood's full work to seal hedges of protection over my households, marriages, generational legacies and dreams - no devil can penetrate this coverage!

164. By this redeeming blood, I cancel out all distractions attempting to bombard my attention away from accomplishing Kingdom priorities. The blood is my focus lens!

165. Through this covenant, I establish spiritual "no-fly" and "no trespass" zones over industries and societal sectors where enemy principalities have tried operating unchallenged.

166. I smear the doorposts of my endeavors with this blood, establishing spiritual quarantines prohibiting demonic behavior, unclean manifestations or contaminations from sabotaging success.

167. I lose angels on assignment of divine guardians, their duty will be escorting and enforcing perimeters established by this sacrificial covenant blood of Jesus.

168. By prophetic decree I create bloodlines defining realms of security permitting only that which carries resurrection life access while prohibiting any death-resonances attempting to cross.

169. As a Blood-washed overcomer, I break the addiction of fear and unbelief, intimidation or defeat from Lucifer's threats or Accusations by taking cover under the blood's unchanging promises.

170. I establish 360 degrees covering of this same blood over my generational legacy marking my family as "off limits" from Hell's attacks, devouring forces or failure to inherit full destiny.

CHAPTER 18
COMMANDING ANGELS TO ASSIST IN BUSINESS AFFAIRS

From Genesis to Revelation, the Scriptures provide an unobstructed witness to the ministry of angels surrounding and assisting God's people in affairs of life and business. Whether it was the Angel of the Lord leading the patriarchs to wells and properties in their nomadic journeys, or ministering spirits accompanying Lot and his family to safety from Sodom's destruction, angels have always been operational in the earthly affairs of Heaven's ambassadors.

As we study entrepreneurial icons like Abraham, Jacob, and Joseph, we find their lives replete with angelic interventions securing deals, providing strategic intelligence on market conditions, and accelerating their business growth to rise above all contemporaries in their realms of commerce and trade. So prominent was this angelic factor that Jacob could proclaim, "The Angel who has redeemed me from all evil, bless the lads" (Genesis 48:16).

Fast forward to the New Testament, and angelic ministry becomes even more prominent, with Jesus Himself affirming that His disciples access angelic reinforcements by mere commanding (Matthew 18:10). From the heavenly hosts celebrating revivals to angels stirring waters for healing, from prison breaks to the rolling away of cosmic stones, we see angels energized for undergirding the church's expansion and supporting emerging business ventures.

Today's entrepreneurial leaders engaged in extending Christ's dominion mandate through business as mission cannot afford to remain unaware of the awesome capacities of angel armies, readily available to assist at a moment's notice. From cutting multi-million-dollar deals, to providing breakthrough strategies, to ensuring financial provision, angels are prepared to work in tandem with you as you learn to cooperate intentionally with them by faith declarations.

This chapter activates your ability to recognize and release angels around matters of enterprise development, marketplace influence and Spirit-inspired initiatives that advance God's Kingdom on earth. As you decree these revelatory prayers, expect to experience accelerated growth trajectories, miraculous open doors, and unstoppable

momentum over endeavors as these messengers go to work for you!

Key Lessons

1. Angels Work Interdependently with God's Entrepreneurs - From biblical patriarchs to modern business vessels for Christ, angels are assigned to work with Spirit-led business leaders expanding Kingdom influence.

2. Angels Accelerate Growth and Provision - Tasked with responsibilities involving acceleration, favor, breakthrough, angelic workforces exponentially increase output and resource flows.

3. Angels Deal in Specifics - Don't issue generic commands; thoroughly detail angelic assignments concerning your unique situations, projects or territories requiring intervention.

4. Angels Follow Christ's Voice Through You As an external reference point of Christ's voice, angels await your authoritative commands to initiate their strategic moves.

5. Angels Navigate the Unseen Realm - Many entrepreneurial hindrances can only be solved through spiritual forces dismantling unseen obstacles angels uniquely discern.

UNCOMMON PRAYERS
Prayers.171-180

171. I call forth angelic hosts and ministering spirits tasked with assisting entrepreneurial assignments for extending Christ's Kingdom through business as mission!

172. I dispatch workforce battalions of angels to provide divine reinforcements accelerating our growth initiatives through

supernatural increase, strategic connections and provision transfers.

173. I summon angels of entrepreneurial revelation, innovation and creativity assisting in the birthing of products, services and delivery systems transforming industries and societies.

174. For territory mapping and establishing new operations, I mobilize battalions of angel armies to map out and overthrow opposition, securing geographical strongholds for Kingdom economic advance.

175. Over sales and client acquisition efforts, I lose angels prospering my business through miraculous favor and unlikely open doors with maximum efficiency.

176. For financial breakthroughs in funding or cash flow increases, I loose Prospering Angels unlocking floodgates and channels of provision from unperceived heavenly sources.

177. Angels of Wisdom and Foresight are engaged to guide my strategic planning, legal affairs and protection over intellectual property and enterprise innovations.

178. I now secure angels of protection over my key assets, properties, staff, transportation and overall operations to maintain sealed environments of security and safety.

179. All demonic harassment against this work through affliction, delay or inefficiency is overruled as I command angels to overwhelm strongholds resisting progress.

180. I establish this business enterprise as a hub in the invisible war between the Kingdom of God and the kingdom of darkness - may mighty hosts of angels now be entrusted to us!

CHAPTER 19
REBUKING SATANIC HARASSMENT IN THE WORKPLACE

While the world often attributes workplace conflict, tension and harassment to personality clashes, broken systems or stressed environments, the truth is much more sobering: demonic forces are actively involved in fomenting disruption, chaos and a plethora of counterattacks specifically targeting businesses and organizations stewarding Kingdom impact and righteousness.

From the very opening scenes in Scripture, we witness Satan faithfully executing his agenda as a workplace harassment specializing in crippling productivity and sowing confusion. Having been banished from his prestigious office as worship leader in Heaven, the adversary slithered into humanity's place of business - Eden - with a vengeance, deceiving man into disobedience then introducing the curses of interpersonal conflict, toil and divine alienation so endemic in earthly workplaces today.

Fast forward to the lives of patriarchs like Joseph, and we find Satan's persistent pattern of leveraging authority figures and relationships to assault the visionary call upon God-ordained leaders in their work environments. Sold into slavery then repeatedly accused, Joseph endured years of setback attacks focused on driving him from destiny until divine intervention reversed his captivity.

Even the apostles within the early church movement were not exempt, enduring harassment tactics like imprisonments, public beatings, and conspiracy plots from adversarial powers determined to abort spiritual awakenings penetrating society's workplaces.

Today, pioneering business leaders and organizations committed to representing Christ's liberation in the workplace remain squarely in the crosshairs of satanic disruption. From seemingly inexplicable people management issues to teams plagued by disunity and misalignment, frequent bouts of adversity often signal more than just natural problems, but possible demonic involvement attempting to undermine vision through workplace strife.

The focused prayers in this chapter pronounce Holy Spirit wisdom to supernaturally detect the adversary's involvement and activity pinpointing spiritual sources of distress over work environments. Through revelatory decrees and militant intercession, you will smash demonic entanglements, bind harassment strategies while losing teams into new realms of redemptive productivity, divine favor and enterprise alignment. Get ready to retake your workplace for His Kingdom purposes!

Key Lessons:

1. The Workplace Was Satan's First Battleground - Since Eden humanity's divinely-ordained place of fruitful labor has been preyed upon by demonic disruption.

2. Spiritual Principality Spirits Focus Specifically on Workplace Harassment - Satan deploys high-ranking territorial principalities whose specialty is obstructing productivity and operations through temper tantrums of harassment, confusion and chaos.

3. Disunity on Teams Signals Possible Spiritual Attacks - Frequent instances of workplace conflict, backstabbing and power struggles often have supernatural roots

rather than just personality or system issues.

4. Setbacks Are Tools for Destiny Delay and Derailment - The adversary uses repeated delays, setbacks and failures to wear down vision and purpose over time.

5. Reversals Propel Advancement - God allows satanic harassment to test resolve and catalyze crisis-level encounters where decisive verdicts are established over the powers of Hell.

UNCOMMON PRAYERS
Prayers.181-190

181. I permanently revoke all satanic squatters, demonic specters and unclean entities harassing this workplace environment and command their instant relocation to the abyss!

182. Through authoritative decrees I demolish and dismantle ruling principalities, strongholds and hostile agendas established by enemy forces to disrupt operations.

183. I forcefully bind the spirits of confusion, miscommunication, disunity and misalignment intentionally deployed to inflict team dysfunctions and operational inefficiencies.

184. Any relationships or individuals currently being leveraged by demonic entities as access points for introducing sabotage, delay or harassment, are now rendered completely off limits by the blood of Jesus!

185. I cancel the assignment of dream killers speaking negative prophetic words attempting to reinforce limiting mindsets, doubt and workplace unbelief regarding this Kingdom vision.

186. I prophetically dismantle all setbacks and reverses sent to obstruct progress by enforcing whiplash season of decreed accelerated advancement and record-shattering achievement!

187. I shatter all curses of failure, mistakes, lawsuits or losses intended to orphan sustainability as generational seeds of blessing are now reassigned to overwhelm opposition.

188. Through authoritative decrees I demolish and dismantle ruling principalities, strongholds and hostile agendas established by enemy forces to disrupt operations

189. I cancel the assignment of dream killers speaking negative prophetic words attempting to reinforce limiting mindsets, doubt and workplace unbelief regarding this Kingdom vision.

CHAPTER 20

DETONATING THE DYNAMITE OF DIVINE INCREASE – PRAYERS FOR EXPLOSIVE SALES AND PROFITABILITY

A **Story of Divine Multiplication:** Imagine the scene: a young David, facing the formidable Goliath. Yet, his unwavering faith empowers him to approach the battle with a simple slingshot and five smooth stones. Against all odds, David's aim finds its mark, toppling the giant and securing a resounding victory for his people. In the realm of business, explosive sales and profitability can feel like a similar David-and-Goliath scenario. But what if you, like David, wielded a weapon far more potent than mere strategy?

Enter the power of prayer.

The story of Elisha (2 Kings 4:1-7) exemplifies the miraculous power of God to multiply resources. Faced with a widow drowning in debt, Elisha instructs her to gather all her vessels. Then, with a simple prayer, he commands oil to flow from a single jar, filling vessel after vessel until they overflow. This widow, empowered by faith, not only settles her debts but thrives.

Contemporary Echoes:
In today's competitive marketplace, countless stories echo these biblical themes. We see small businesses, fueled by prayer and a deep trust in God's provision, flourishing against industry giants. We witness sales teams, empowered by unwavering faith, exceeding targets and forging enduring client relationships.

Key Lessons

1. Profitability is a Divine Gift: Recognize that financial success is not solely a product of human effort, but a blessing bestowed by God.

2. Faith Activates Abundance: Your unwavering belief in God's plan for your business opens the door to overflowing blessings.

3. Gratitude is the Fuel: Expressing sincere appreciation for every sale and every customer magnifies your prosperity.

4. Ethical Conduct is the Foundation: Building trust and integrity into your

business practices paves the way for sustainable growth.

5.Generosity Breeds Abundance: Opening your heart to give back fosters a spirit of abundance that attracts further blessings.

UNCOMMON PRAYERS

for Explosive Sales and Profitability: Prayers. 191-200

191. Heavenly Father, I surrender the pursuit of profit to your will. Guide my steps towards ethical and sustainable growth.

192. Lord, break any spiritual chains hindering the flow of abundance into my business.

193. I rebuke any negativity or fear that may impede sales and productivity.

194. Grant me wisdom in setting prices, discernment in negotiations, and the power to close deals with integrity.

195. Open the hearts and minds of potential customers, making them receptive to the value I offer.

196. Surround my business with a hedge of protection from dishonest practices and cutthroat competition.

197. I lift up my sales team, empowering them with confidence, creativity, and a spirit of collaboration.

198. Fill my workplace with a contagious enthusiasm that resonates with every customer interaction.

199. Grant me discernment to identify and capitalize on new opportunities for growth and expansion.

200. Above all, I pray for the wisdom to use my prosperity for your glory, to bless others, and honor your name.

CHAPTER 21
BIRTHING NEW STREAMS OF INCOME AND WEALTH - UNVEILING THE WELLSPRING OF ABUNDANCE

A Story of Unexpected Provision: The book of Exodus recounts the Israelites' arduous journey through the wilderness. Facing a parched landscape and the threat of thirst, despair threatened to consume them. Yet, when Moses struck a rock with his staff at God's command (Exodus 17:6), a miraculous spring gushed forth, quenching their desperate need. This story serves as a powerful metaphor for the unexpected ways God can birth new streams of income and wealth for those who trust in Him.

Contemporary Echoes of Abundance:

Just as Moses tapped into a hidden spring, countless entrepreneurs today credit divine intervention for the birth of groundbreaking ideas and unforeseen opportunities. We see individuals with limited resources stumble upon unique market niches, their businesses blossoming into empires. We witness unexpected partnerships forming, leading to lucrative ventures that propel them to new heights of financial security.

The Woman with the Alabaster Flask:
The story of the woman who anointed Jesus' feet with expensive perfume (Mark 14:3-9) offers another perspective. Her seemingly extravagant act of devotion was met with criticism. Yet, Jesus recognized the purity of her heart and the significance of her offering.

This narrative reminds us that when we prioritize honoring God with our resources, He multiplies our blessings in unforeseen ways.

Key Lessons

1. Openness to New Ideas: Cultivate a spirit of openness to new possibilities and creative ventures.

2. Faith Over Fear: Don't be afraid to step outside your comfort zone and pursue ventures rooted in faith.

3. Wise Stewardship: Manage your existing resources responsibly, for faithfulness in the little things precedes greater blessings.

4. The Power of Generosity: Giving back from your heart opens the door for God to multiply your wealth in unexpected ways.

5. Recognizing Divine Opportunities: Develop a keen eye to identify God-given opportunities that may appear unconventional.

UNCOMMON PRAYERS
for Birthing New Streams of Income and Wealth'
Prayers. 201-210

201. Father, open my eyes to see opportunities for new streams of income that align with your will.

202. Grant me the wisdom to discern between fleeting trends and ventures with lasting potential.

203. I break any fear of scarcity that may hinder my ability to pursue new opportunities.

204. Cleanse my heart of greed and entitlement, and replace them with a desire to honor you through my wealth.

205. Surround me with wise advisors and mentors who will guide me on the path to financial prosperity.

206. I cancel any negative financial cycles that have plagued my past, and I declare a season of abundance.

207. I rebuke any spirit of stagnation or lack that may impede the flow of new income streams.

208. Grant me the courage to take calculated risks, trusting in your guidance and provision.

209. Open doors of favor with potential partners and investors who share my values.

210. Above all, I pray that my wealth becomes a tool to bless others, further your kingdom, and glorify your name.

CHAPTER 22
RELEASING BLESSINGS ON EMPLOYEES AND LEADERS

In the bustling business world, a harmonious note often goes unheard - the power of prayer for leaders to release blessings upon their employees and themselves. While strategies, budgets, and deadlines command our attention, the human element – the beating hearts and striving minds that drive success – can be neglected. This chapter delves into the transformative potential of prayer, offering a biblical foundation for leadership that transcends mere efficiency and embraces the spiritual well-being of those entrusted to your care.

The Wellspring of Leadership: Lessons from the Shepherd King

The Bible provides a wealth of wisdom on leadership, and few figures exemplify this wisdom as powerfully as King David. David, a man "after God's own heart" (1 Samuel 13:14), wasn't just a military strategist or a shrewd politician. He was a shepherd at his core, a leader who understood the importance of nurturing and protecting his flock. His Psalms resonate with a deep love and concern for his people, reflecting a leadership style rooted in compassion and care (Psalm 23).

Leaders in today's world, navigating the complexities of the corporate landscape, can glean valuable lessons from David's example. Just as a shepherd prioritizes the well-being of his sheep, so too should leaders prioritize the well-being of their employees. This extends beyond material needs to encompass their emotional, spiritual, and professional growth. By releasing blessings through prayer, leaders cultivate a sense of security, purpose, and belonging within their organization, fostering a more human-centered approach to leadership.

The Ripple Effect: Prayer as a Catalyst for Transformation

Imagine a leader who begins each day with a simple yet profound act: prayer for their employees. They pray not just for success in the next quarter, but for wisdom in decision-making, for creativity and collaboration among teams, and for a spirit of respect and fairness to permeate the workplace. These prayers, seemingly silent and unseen, have a profound ripple effect.

Employees who feel valued, supported, and prayed for are demonstrably more engaged and productive. Studies have shown a positive correlation between employee well-being and organizational success. A leader who releases blessings through prayer fosters a more positive and productive work environment, where individuals feel empowered to reach their full potential. This, in turn, translates into a more innovative, resilient, and ultimately, successful organization.

Beyond Efficiency: Cultivating a Sanctuary of Purpose

Leadership in the contemporary business world often emphasizes efficiency and results. Yet, a singular focus on metrics can leave employees feeling like cogs in a machine, devoid of purpose and connection. Prayer, when practiced by leaders, transcends this transactional approach. It becomes an act of acknowledging the inherent worth of each individual within the organization. By praying for their employees, leaders are essentially saying, "You matter. Your well-being matters. Your contribution matters."

This shift in perspective fosters a sense of purpose within the team. Employees who feel seen, valued, and supported are more likely to approach their work with dedication and a sense of ownership. The workplace transforms from a mere place of employment to a sanctuary of purpose, where individuals can contribute not just their skills, but also their hearts and minds to a shared vision.

A Call to Action

Integrating prayer into your leadership practice requires intentionality and a genuine desire for the well-being of those entrusted to your care. Here are some practical steps to get you started:

Begin Your Day with Prayer: Dedicate a few minutes each morning to pray for your employees. Ask for wisdom in your leadership, for creativity and collaboration within the team, and for a spirit of respect and fairness to prevail.

Embrace Specific Prayers: Tailor your prayers to address specific needs within your organization. Pray for struggling team members, for upcoming challenges, and for the professional development of your employees.

Lead by Example: Don't be afraid to share your faith with your team in an authentic way. Discuss the importance of prayer in your leadership and encourage them to incorporate spiritual practices into their own lives.

Create a Culture of Support: Foster a work environment where employees feel comfortable discussing personal challenges and seeking support from colleagues and leaders.

Celebrate Victories, Big and Small: Give thanks for accomplishments, both individual and collective. This cultivates a spirit of gratitude and motivates the team to strive for continued growth.

By incorporating these practices, you can become a leader who not only commands respect but also inspires devotion. Your leadership transforms into a harmonious symphony, where prayer serves as the foundational melody, guiding your team towards professional success and personal fulfillment. Remember, the most effective leaders are those who recognize that true leadership extends beyond the bottom line.

Key Lessons

1. Leadership as Stewardship: Shift your perspective from leader as commander to leader as shepherd. Your role is to guide, protect, and nurture the well-being of your employees.

2. The Power of Prayer in Action: Prayer is not a passive act; it's a catalyst for positive change. By praying for your employees, you release blessings that foster a more positive and productive work environment.

3. Beyond Efficiency: Cultivating Purpose: Move beyond a purely transactional approach to leadership. Help your employees discover meaning and purpose in their work, fostering a sense of ownership and dedication.

4. The Ripple Effect of Blessings: The positive impact of your prayers extends beyond yourself. It empowers employees, fosters collaboration, and ultimately contributes to organizational success.

5. Leading by Example: Don't be afraid to integrate your faith into your leadership style. By sharing your values and practices authentically, you inspire a more human-centered approach to business.

UNCOMMON PRAYERS
Prayers. 201-210

201. For Wisdom and Guidance: "Almighty God, grant me the wisdom of Solomon in leading my team. Guide me in making decisions that are both strategic and compassionate." (Proverbs 2:6)

202. For Innovation and Collaboration: "Holy Spirit, breathe your creativity into our team meetings. Help us to break down silos, brainstorm new ideas, and find innovative solutions together." (Ephesians 4:16)

203. For a Respectful Work Environment: "Lord, cultivate an atmosphere of mutual respect and understanding within our

workplace. Guide us in resolving conflicts with grace and integrity." (Colossians 3:13)

204. For Overcoming Obstacles: "God, when challenges arise, equip our team with resilience and perseverance. Grant us the strength to navigate difficulties with wisdom and emerge stronger." (James 1:2-4)

205. For a Culture of Gratitude: "Dear Father, we give thanks for the successes we achieve together. Help us to celebrate each other's accomplishments and cultivate a spirit of appreciation within our team." (1 Thessalonians 5:18)

Prayers for Employee Growth and Success:

206. For Motivation and Fulfillment: "Heavenly Father, ignite a passion for excellence within my employees. Help them find joy and fulfillment in the tasks they perform." (Proverbs 16:9)

207. For Skill Development: "Lord, open doors of opportunity for my employees to learn and grow in their chosen fields. Guide them towards valuable resources and mentors." (Proverbs 22:29)

208. For Work-Life Balance: "God, grant my employees the wisdom to manage their time effectively and achieve a healthy

balance between work and personal life." (Exodus 33:14)

209. For Overcoming Personal Challenges: "Almighty God, when my employees face personal struggles, surround them with your love and support. Guide them towards resources and strength to navigate challenging times." (Psalm 91:4)

210. For a Positive Work Ethic: "Holy Spirit, instill a spirit of dedication and excellence within my team. Motivate them to perform their best in all they do, for the benefit of themselves and the organization." (Colossians 3:23-24)

CHAPTER 23
FINDING SANCTUARY IN THE WHIRLWIND – PRAYERS FOR WORK-LIFE BALANCE AND PRIORITIES

A Story of Sabbath Rest:
Throughout the book of Exodus, God emphasizes the importance of Sabbath rest, a day dedicated to stepping away from work and refocusing on Him (Exodus 20:8-11). This principle of intentional rest is as relevant today as ever for the busy executive. It's a reminder that neglecting your personal well-being ultimately hinders your professional success.

Contemporary Echoes of Balance:

The "always-on" culture of the modern world can leave executives feeling perpetually drained. Yet, a growing trend sees successful leaders prioritizing work-life balance. They recognize the importance of setting boundaries, delegating tasks, and disconnecting to recharge. Studies show that leaders who prioritize personal well-being return to work with renewed focus, creativity, and resilience.

The Parable of the Sower:

The parable of the Sower (Matthew 13:1-9) offers valuable insight. The seeds sown on fertile ground represent priorities that receive our focused attention and yield a bountiful harvest. The seeds scattered on the path or choked by weeds symbolize tasks neglected due to a lack of prioritization. This parable reminds us that neglecting our personal well-being is like neglecting fertile soil - our productivity suffers.

Key Lessons:
1. Prioritize ruthlessly: Learn to say no to requests that don't align with your core values and goals.

2. Embrace the Power of Delegation: Empower your team by delegating tasks effectively.

3. Schedule Disconnection: Block out time in your calendar for rest, relaxation, and connecting with loved ones.

4. Sabbath for Success: Dedicate uninterrupted time for spiritual renewal, even if it's not a traditional Sunday.

5. Guard Your Energy: Identify activities that drain your energy and replace them with practices that replenish your spirit.

UNCOMMON PRAYER for Work-Life Balance and Priorities: Prayers 211-220

211. Heavenly Father, grant me the wisdom to discern between urgent tasks and those that can wait.

212. I break the chains of workaholism and the pressure to be constantly "on."

213. Help me delegate tasks effectively and empower my team to take ownership.

214. Grant me the discipline to stick to my schedule, including dedicated time for rest and family.

215. Show me creative ways to integrate moments of prayer and reflection into my busy day.

216. I rebuke any guilt or anxiety associated with taking time for myself and my loved ones.

217. Help me identify and eliminate activities that deplete my energy and emotional well-being.

218. Guide me towards creating a work environment that promotes healthy work-life boundaries for all.

219. Grant me the grace to say no to requests that would compromise my personal well-being.

220. Above all, help me trust that by honoring Your call to rest and prioritize my wholeness, I ultimately become a more effective leader and a more fulfilled human being.

CHAPTER 24
CONQUERING THE GIANTS WITHIN - OVERCOMING ANXIETY, STRESS, AND BURNOUT

A Story of Trust and Surrender:
The book of Psalms offers a treasure trove of prayers for those facing overwhelming burdens. In Psalm 55, King David, a man familiar with stress and anxiety, pours out his heart to God, seeking refuge and strength (Psalm 55:1-22). This raw honesty and act of surrender serve as a powerful reminder that even the most successful leaders need moments of

vulnerability and reliance on a higher power.

Contemporary Echoes of Overcoming: The relentless pressure to perform can leave even the most seasoned executive vulnerable to anxiety, stress, and burnout. However, a growing number of leaders are breaking the silence and advocating for mental well-being. They openly discuss their struggles and champion practices like mindfulness meditation and therapy, demonstrating that strength lies not in stoicism, but in vulnerability and proactive self-care.

The Parable of the Lost Sheep:

The parable of the lost sheep (Luke 15:3-7) offers a comforting message. The shepherd leaves the ninety-nine secure sheep to search for the one lost. This parable reminds us that God's love and concern extend even to the most stressed and burnt-out leader. He doesn't expect us to carry the weight of the world alone.

Key Lessons
1. Acknowledge the Burden: Ignoring stress and anxiety will only exacerbate them. Be honest with yourself and seek help when needed.

2. Prioritize Self-Care: Schedule time for activities that nourish your mind, body, and spirit.

3. Embrace Vulnerability: Talking openly about your struggles can be liberating and foster a supportive network.

4. Seek Professional Help: Therapy can equip you with tools to manage stress and cultivate emotional resilience.

5. Surrender and Trust: Release the need for complete control and place your faith in God's sustaining power.

UNCOMMON PRAYERS for Overcoming Anxiety, Stress, and Burnout.
Prayers 221-230

221. Dear Heavenly Father, I confess the burden of stress and anxiety that weighs me down.

222. I break the cycle of worry and surrender my anxieties to your loving care.

223. Grant me the wisdom to identify the root causes of my stress and burnout.

224. Show me healthy ways to manage my workload and delegate tasks effectively.

225. Guide me towards creating a work-life balance that promotes peace and rejuvenation.

6. I rebuke any spirit of fear or negativity that seeks to paralyze me.

227. Fill me with Your peace that transcends all understanding, even in the midst of challenges.

228. Lead me to supportive resources and professionals who can guide me towards healing and wholeness.

229. Grant me the strength to set healthy boundaries and prioritize my well-being.

230. Above all, remind me that I am not alone in this battle. You are my refuge and my strength, a very present help in trouble.

CHAPTER 25
CONSECRATING BUSINESS FOR KINGDOM PURPOSES - BUILDING AN EMPIRE FOR HIS GLORY

A Story of Purpose Beyond Profit: The book of Proverbs is filled with wisdom on conducting business ethically and with integrity (Proverbs 11:1, 16:8). Yet, it also reminds us that true success goes beyond material wealth. In Proverbs 3:9-10, we are called to honor God with our first fruits, a metaphor for prioritizing His will above personal gain. This principle of consecration extends to our businesses, calling us to use them as instruments for His glory.

Contemporary Echoes of Kingdom Businesses:

A growing number of entrepreneurs are choosing to operate their businesses with a higher purpose in mind. They integrate ethical practices, social responsibility, and faith-based values into their operations. These "Kingdom businesses" prioritize not just profit, but also creating a positive impact on their communities, employees, and the environment. They demonstrate that financial success and social responsibility can coexist, creating a ripple effect of positive change.

The Parable of the Talents (Reprise)

The parable of the talents (Matthew 25:14-30) takes on a new dimension in this context. The servants who invest their talents and multiply their wealth are commended for being good stewards. However, in the context of Kingdom businesses, the "investment" extends beyond financial gain. It encompasses using our resources to build a company that reflects God's values, serves the community, and honors Him.

Key Lessons

1. Beyond the Bottom Line: Seek to integrate your faith and values into your business practices.

2. Social Responsibility: Use your business platform to create a positive impact on the world.

3. Ethical Leadership: Lead with integrity, fairness, and a commitment to the well-being of all stakeholders.

4. Generosity Beyond Profit: Incorporate charitable giving and community service into your business model.

5. Celebrating Success with Gratitude: Recognize that your achievements are ultimately blessings from God, to be used for His glory.

UNCOMMON PRAYERS for Consecrating Business for Kingdom Purposes.
Prayers 231-240

231. Heavenly Father, I consecrate this business to you. May it be a tool to advance Your kingdom and bring glory to Your name.

232. I break any spirit of greed or self-promotion that may seek to overshadow Your purpose for this company.

233. Grant me wisdom to make decisions that align with biblical principles of justice, fairness, and compassion.

234. Guide me in attracting employees who share my values and contribute to building a positive work environment.

235. Open doors to opportunities that allow us to use our resources to bless others and serve our community.

236. I rebuke any negativity or dishonesty that may threaten the integrity of this business.

237 Grant me the courage to stand firm in my faith, even in a competitive marketplace.

238 Help us cultivate a culture of generosity within the company, inspiring employees to give back.

239. Grant me discernment to recognize and resist unethical practices that may lead to financial gain but compromise your principles.

240. Above all, may this business be a beacon of hope, reflecting Your love and serving as a force for good in the world.

CONCLUSION
From Prayers to Powerhouse Performance - Your Journey to Uncommon Success Begins Now

As you reach the final page of BREAKTHROUGH! 120 UNCOMMON PRAYERS FOR BUSINESS EXECUTIVES, a powerful transformation awaits. These prayers weren't simply words on paper. They were seeds, carefully planted in the fertile ground of your ambition and faith. Now, it's time to nurture those seeds and witness them blossom into a harvest of remarkable achievements.

Remember, this book is not an ending, but a potent beginning. You've explored the power of scripture in the context of modern business challenges. You've discovered the

secret weapon wielded by countless successful leaders - unwavering faith and a fervent prayer life. But true mastery lies in action.

CALL FOR ACTION

1. Personalize Your Prayers:
The prayers in this book are springboards. Take them, personalize them, and make them your own. Speak directly to God from your heart, expressing your deepest desires, fears, and dreams for your business.

2. Integrate Prayer into Your Routine:

Carve out dedicated time for prayer, whether in the quiet moments of the morning or before crucial meetings. Make prayer a constant companion, a guiding force in every decision you make.

3. Start a Prayer Group:
Gather a trusted group of colleagues who share your faith and create a prayer circle specifically for your business endeavors. Uplift and support each other on this journey.

4. Share the Power of Prayer:
Don't be afraid to share your faith and the power of prayer with others. Encourage colleagues, mentors, and business partners to join you on this transformative journey. Together, create a ripple effect of faith in your professional sphere.

5. Declare Your Faith Publicly:

Consider incorporating a mission statement that reflects your faith-based values into your company's website or marketing materials. Let your commitment to ethical practices and social responsibility be known.

6. Track Your Breakthroughs:
As you integrate prayer into your business practices, keep a journal to document your victories and challenges. Witnessing answered prayers fosters an unshakeable belief in the power of faith to propel you forward.

7. Become a Mentor:
As you experience success, pay it forward by mentoring other aspiring faith-based

entrepreneurs. Share your experiences, challenges, and triumphs, and inspire the next generation of leaders.

8. Give Back Generously:
Let your success be a blessing to others. Integrate philanthropy into your business model, supporting causes you care about and demonstrating your commitment to social responsibility.

9. Advocate for Ethical Practices:
Use your voice to promote ethical conduct and fair treatment for all stakeholders within your industry. Be a beacon of integrity in the marketplace.

10. Embrace Continuous Learning:
Never stop learning and growing as a leader. Explore additional resources on faith-driven leadership, attend workshops,

and stay connected with the growing community of Christian business leaders.

Remember, you are not alone on this journey. Countless business leaders, armed with faith and fueled by prayer, have achieved remarkable success. You, too, can join their ranks.

Embrace the power of **BREAKTHROUGH!** Embrace the power of prayer. Embrace the potential for uncommon success that lies within you. Go forth, lead with faith, and watch your business soar to unimaginable heights.

Additional Resources:

This book is just the beginning of your exploration of faith and business. We encourage you to delve deeper! Consider joining online communities of faith-based entrepreneurs, attending workshops on faith-driven leadership, or exploring inspirational literature in this growing field.

Together, let us rewrite the narrative of business. Let us show the world the extraordinary achievements possible when faith meets action.

www.ingramcontent.com/pod-product-compliance
Lightning Source LLC
Chambersburg PA
CBHW052148220526
45471CB00004B/1584